MORE LETTERS OF
# OSCAR WILDE

# MORE LETTERS OF
# OSCAR WILDE

*Edited by*

RUPERT HART-DAVIS

John Murray

First published 1985
by John Murray (Publishers) Ltd
50 Albemarle Street, London W1X 4BD

Typeset by Keyspeed Typesetting Co., Leigh, Lancs
Printed and bound in Great Britain
by the Bath Press, Bath


British Library CIP Data
Wilde, Oscar
More letters of Oscar Wilde.
1. Wilde, Oscar——Biography
2. Authors, Irish——19th century——Biography
I. Title    II. Hart-Davis, Rupert
828'.809    PR5823
ISBN 0-7195-4174-3

*This book is dedicated
by its editor
with affection
to Merlin and Lucian Holland
grandson and great-grandson
of Oscar Wilde*

# CONTENTS

THE HAND OF OSCAR WILDE

A photograph of Oscar Wilde's palm appears on page 187.

# INTRODUCTION

*The Letters of Oscar Wilde* first appeared in 1962, when it went through four printings. Now it has long been out of print, though many of the best letters can be found in the Oxford paperback *Selected Letters of Oscar Wilde*, which is still available.

Since 1962 more than two hundred further letters have come to light. Of them the 164 in this book are the only interesting ones: the others are trivial notes, always undated, often to unidentifiable people.

To the 164 I have added the full text of ten letters that appeared in abbreviated form in *The Letters* (there are eight others with better texts in *Selected Letters*); also, in their chronological places, seven letters to Wilde, and two about him, which fill in gaps and add extra details to this ever-fascinating life.

In fact the whole of this book does just that. It must be largely considered as a supplement to *The Letters*, but I have done my best to make it in a small way self-contained. I have included some references to *The Letters*, but recurring individuals who were fully footnoted there are here given brief notes only. New characters are fully noted. As before, I have corrected Wilde's spelling and regularised his punctuation. I have retained the nine divisions of *The Letters*, each bearing the name of the place where Wilde spent most of that period. All the main dates of his life are in the Biographical Table on pp. 15–19. In the index the first page-number after each person's name indicates the position of his or her main biographical particulars.

No doubt many other letters will turn up over the years, but it seems sensible to print this lot while I am still here to do it.

Letters headed "TS. Congress" and "TS. Clark" are typescript copies made by Wilde's bibliographer Stuart Mason, who was a careful transcriber. When Mr Donald J. Kaufmann acquired the letters to Norman Forbes-Robertson and kindly sent me photo-copies, their texts were identical with those I had printed in *The Letters* as TS. Congress.

Reference to MS. in headnote or elsewhere means that I have seen the original or a photo-copy. "MS. Private" means that I have seen the original or a photo-copy, but the present owner is unknown or prefers to remain anonymous.

The following abbreviations are used in the footnotes:

Mason        *Bibliography of Oscar Wilde* by Stuart Mason (1914). A photographic reprint was published in 1967.

*Miscellanies* Volume XIV of the Collected Edition of Wilde's works, edited by Robert Ross (1908).

*Reviews*      Volume XIII of the Collected Edition (1908).

I owe many debts of gratitude, and the greatest of them is to Mrs Mary Hyde. She now has far and away the largest and best collection of Wilde letters, manuscripts and other material in private hands. She has carried on the kindness and generosity that she and her husband Donald showed me when I was editing *The Letters*, and over the years since Donald's death she has continued to send me photo-copies of all her new acquisitions, besides answering many tiresome questions. Without her and Donald's help these two books would have been poor indeed. My gratitude to them both is unbounded.

I have always been indebted to the William Andrews

Clark Library in the University of California at Los Angeles, and they too have generously sent me copies of new letters. In particular I render thanks to Mr William E. Conway, the recently retired Librarian.

Mr Frederick R. Koch has now entered the lists as a leading Wilde collector. He has given most of his collection to the Pierpont Morgan Library in New York, and for photo-copies I send my thanks to him and to my old friend Herbert Cahoon of the Morgan Library.

I am deeply grateful to all the other private owners who have sent me photo-copies of their letters, and for various other help and kindness I owe much gratitude to Mr Nicolas Barker; Professor Joseph O. Baylen of Georgia State University, Atlanta; Dr Robert Becker; Professor Karl Beckson of Brooklyn College, New York; Mr Alan Bell; Dr Richard Bingle of the India Office Records; Miss Edra Bogle; Mr Paul Chipchase; Dr Noel J. Cortes; Mr Paul Delaney; Professor Vic Doyno of the State University, Buffalo; Mr Clive E. Driver of the Rosenbach Foundation; The Rev. Francis O. Edwards, S.J; Professor Richard Ellmann of Oxford University; Mr Lawrence Evans; Mr Marc S. Gallicchio of the Historical Society of Pennsylvania; Mr Richard and Mr Roger Lancelyn Green; Mr Richard Halverson; Mr Robert Jackson; Mr Michael Jamieson; Mr Ralph Kane; Mrs Marjory Kilburn; Mr Dan H. Laurence; Mr James Morwood of the Vaughan Library, Harrow School; the staff of the National Library of Scotland; Mr Simon Nowell-Smith; Professor Kevin O'Brien of St Francis Xavier University, Antigonish, Nova Scotia; Mr Frank Paluka of the University of Iowa; the late Mr Mike Papantonio of the Seven Gables Bookshop, New York; Mrs Carol Patterson; Mr Richard Pine of Trinity College, Dublin; Professor Ellis M. Pryce-Jones; Lord Ravensdale; Miss Nancy Ann Rogers; Mr Kenneth Rose; Miss Barbara J. Schaller of the Lynn Public Library; Mrs Dorothy

11

Lockhart Smith; Mr John Sparrow; Mrs Delia Taylor of Queen Mary College; Miss Molly Thomas of the Ellen Terry Memorial Museum; and Professor J. Walker of Queen's University, Ontario.

A great deal of my footnote-research has been done by my indefatigable and highly skilled old friend Ernest Mehew, ably assisted by his wife Joyce. They have also relentlessly scrutinised the proofs, as have Paul Chipchase and the other two experts who helped me more than twenty years ago — Henry Maas and Owen Dudley Edwards. This book and its predecessor owe an enormous lot to all of them, and I am hopelessly and forever in their debt. Lastly, and above all, Merlin Holland has trusted and encouraged me, as his father Vyvyan did in the past, and I record my affectionate gratitude to them both. There must be others who have helped me since 1962, but old men forget, and I can only gratefully beg the forgiveness of any such neglected benefactors.

*Marske-in-Swaledale*                    RUPERT HART-DAVIS


*Postscript.* Since I wrote the above Mrs Mary Hyde has become the Viscountess Eccles. I send her my joyful felicitations and unending gratitude.   R.H-D.

# MANUSCRIPT LOCATIONS

## 1. *Institutions*

| | |
|---|---|
| Bodleian | Oxford University Archives in the Bodleian Library |
| Buffalo | State University of New York, Buffalo |
| Chichester | West Sussex Record Office, Chichester |
| Clark | William Andrews Clark Library, Los Angeles |
| Cleveland | Western Reserve University Libraries, Cleveland, Ohio |
| Colgate | Colgate University, New York |
| Congress | Library of Congress, Washington, D.C. |
| Curzon | Curzon Collection in the India Office Library |
| Dalhousie | Dalhousie University Library, Halifax, Nova Scotia |
| Dallas | Dallas Public Library, Texas |
| Edinburgh | National Library of Scotland, Edinburgh |
| Erie | Buffalo & Erie Public Library |
| Harrow | Vaughan Library, Harrow School |
| Lockwood | Lockwood Memorial Library, Buffalo |
| Montague | Montague Collection, New York Public Library |
| Morgan | Pierpont Morgan Library, New York |
| NYPL | Rare Book Department, New York Public Library |
| Pennsylvania | Historical Society of Pennsylvania, Philadelphia |
| Prague | Narodniho Musea, Prague |
| Princeton | Princeton University Library |
| QMC | Queen Mary College, University of London |
| Rosenbach | Rosenbach Foundation, Philadelphia |

| | |
|---|---|
| Smallhythe | Ellen Terry Memorial Museum, Smallhythe, Kent |
| Texas | Humanities Research Center, Austin, Texas |

## 2. *Private Owners*

| | |
|---|---|
| Burgunder | Mr Bernard Burgunder |
| Grenfell | The Grenfell Papers, in care of Lord Ravensdale |
| Hatfield | Hatfield House, Hertfordshire |
| Hyde | Mrs Donald Hyde |
| Jestin | Mr & Mrs H.B. Jestin |
| Kaufmann | Mr Donald J. Kaufmann |
| Koch | Mr Frederick R. Koch |
| MacManus | Mr George S. MacManus |
| Macmillan | Mr W.G. Macmillan |
| Maguire | Mr J. Robert Maguire |
| Mason | Mr Jeremy Mason |
| Taylor | The Robert H. Taylor Collection at Princeton |

# BIOGRAPHICAL TABLE

| 1854 | October 16 | Oscar Wilde born at 21 Westland Row, Dublin |
|------|------------|---------------------------------------------|
| 1855 | | Family moves to 1 Merrion Square North |
| 1864–71 | | At Portora Royal School, Enniskillen |
| 1871–74 | | At Trinity College, Dublin |
| 1874 | October | Goes up to Magdalen College, Oxford, as Demy |
| 1875 | June | Travels in Italy with Mahaffy |
| 1876 | April 19 | Death of Sir William Wilde |
| | July 5 | First in Mods |
| 1877 | March–April | Visits Greece with Mahaffy, returning *via* Rome |
| 1878 | June 10 | Wins Newdigate Prize with *Ravenna* |
| | July 19 | First in Greats |
| | November 28 | B.A. degree |
| 1879 | Autumn | Takes rooms with Frank Miles at 13 Salisbury Street, London |
| 1880 | August | Moves with Miles to Keats House, Tite Street, Chelsea |
| 1881 | June ?30 | *Poems* published |
| | December 24 | Embarks for U.S.A. |
| 1882 | | Lectures in U.S.A. and Canada all the year |
| 1883 | January–?May | In Paris, Hôtel Voltaire |

| | | |
|---|---|---|
| | ?July | Moves into rooms at 9 Charles Street, Grosvenor Square |
| | Aug–Sept | Visits New York briefly for production of *Vera* |
| | September 24 | Begins lecture-tour in U.K., which lasts off and on for a year |
| | November 26 | Engaged to Constance Lloyd |
| 1884 | May 29 | Married to Constance Lloyd in London |
| | May 29–June 24 | On honeymoon in Paris and Dieppe |
| 1885 | January 1 | Moves into 16 Tite Street |
| | June 5 | Cyril Wilde born |
| 1886 | | Meets Robert Ross |
| | November 3 | Vyvyan Wilde born |
| 1887 | | Begins editorship of the *Woman's World* |
| 1888 | May | *The Happy Prince and other Tales* published |
| 1889 | July | Brief visit to Kreuznach "The Portrait of Mr W.H." published in *Blackwood's* |
| | October | Gives up editorship of the *Woman's World* |
| 1890 | June 20 | *The Picture of Dorian Gray* published in *Lippincott's* |
| 1891 | ?January | Meets Lord Alfred Douglas |
| | January | *The Duchess of Padua* produced in New York as *Guido Ferranti* |
| | February | *The Soul of Man under Socialism* published in *Fortnightly* |
| | April | *The Picture of Dorian Gray* published in book form |
| | May 2 | *Intentions* published |
| | July | *Lord Arthur Savile's Crime and Other Stories* published |
| | November | *A House of Pomegranates* published |
| | Nov–Dec | Writes *Salome* in Paris |

| 1892 | February 20 | *Lady Windermere's Fan* produced |
| | May 26 | Limited edition of *Poems* published |
| | June | *Salome* banned by Lord Chamberlain |
| | July | Takes cure at Homburg |
| | Aug–Sept | Writes *A Woman of No Importance* in Norfolk |
| | November | Takes Babbacombe Cliff, near Torquay |
| 1893 | February 22 | *Salome* published in French |
| | March 5 | Leaves Babbacombe |
| | April 19 | *A Woman of No Importance* produced |
| | June–October | At The Cottage, Goring-on-Thames |
| | October | Takes rooms at 10 and 11 St James's Place. Writes *An Ideal Husband* there |
| | November 9 | *Lady Windermere's Fan* published |
| 1894 | February 9 | *Salome* published in English, illustrated by Beardsley |
| | May | In Florence with Douglas |
| | June 11 | *The Sphinx* published |
| | Aug–Sept | Writes *The Importance of Being Earnest* at Worthing |
| | October 9 | *A Woman of No Importance* published |
| | October | At Brighton with Douglas |
| 1895 | January 3 | *An Ideal Husband* produced |
| | January 17–31 | Visits Algiers with Douglas |
| | February 14 | *The Importance of Being Earnest* produced |
| | February 28 | Finds Queensberry's card at Albemarle Club |
| | March 1 | Obtains warrant for Queensberry's arrest |
| | March 9 | Queensberry remanded at Bow Street for trial at Old Bailey |
| | March | Visits Monte Carlo with Douglas |
| | April 3 | Queensberry trial opens |
| | April 5 | Queensberry acquitted. Wilde arrested |

|            |                 |                                                                          |
|------------|-----------------|--------------------------------------------------------------------------|
|            | April 6–26      | Imprisoned at Holloway                                                    |
|            | April 26        | First trial opens                                                         |
|            | May 1           | Jury disagree. New trial ordered                                          |
|            | May 7           | Released on bail                                                          |
|            | May 20          | Second trial opens                                                        |
|            | May 25          | Sentenced to two years' hard labour and imprisoned (after two days at Newgate) at Pentonville |
|            | July 4          | Transferred to Wandsworth                                                 |
|            | September 24    | First examination in Bankruptcy                                          |
|            | November 12     | Second examination in Bankruptcy                                         |
|            | November 20     | Transferred to Reading                                                   |
| 1896       | February 3      | Death of Lady Wilde                                                      |
|            | February 11     | *Salome* produced in Paris                                               |
| 1897       | January–March   | Writes *De Profundis*                                                    |
|            | May 18          | Transferred to Pentonville                                               |
|            | May 19          | Released. Crosses to Dieppe by night boat                               |
|            | May 26          | Moves from Dieppe to Berneval-sur-Mer                                   |
|            | August ?28–29   | Meets Douglas at Rouen                                                   |
|            | September 4–11  | At Rouen                                                                 |
|            | September 15    | Leaves Dieppe for Paris                                                  |
|            | September 20    | Arrives at Naples                                                        |
|            | September ?27   | Moves to Villa Giudice, Posilippo                                       |
|            | October 15–18   | Visits Capri with Douglas                                               |
|            | December        | Visits Sicily                                                           |
| 1898       | January         | Moves to 31 Santa Lucia, Naples                                         |
|            | February ?13    | Moves to Hôtel de Nice, Paris                                           |
|            | February 13     | *The Ballad of Reading Gaol* published                                  |
|            | March *c*. 28   | Moves to Hôtel d'Alsace                                                 |
|            | April 7         | Death of Constance Wilde                                                |
|            | June–July       | At Nogent-sur-Marne                                                     |
|            | August          | At Chennevières-sur-Marne                                               |
|            | December 15     | Leaves for Napoule, near Cannes                                         |
| 1899       | February        | *The Importance of Being Earnest* published                            |

18

| | | |
|---|---|---|
| | February | Leaves Napoule for Nice |
| | February 25 | Leaves Nice for Gland, Switzerland |
| | April 1 | Leaves Gland for Santa Margherita |
| | April–May | Returns to Paris, Hôtel de la Néva |
| | May | Moves to Hôtel Marsollier |
| | June 23–26 | At Trouville and Le Havre |
| | July | *An Ideal Husband* published |
| | July | At Chennevières-sur-Marne |
| | August | Moves back to Hôtel d'Alsace |
| 1900 | April 2–10 | At Palermo |
| | April 12– | |
| | May ?15 | In Rome |
| | May | Ten days at Gland |
| | May–June | Returns to Paris |
| | October 10 | Operated on |
| | November 30 | Dies in Hôtel d'Alsace |

# OXFORD

## 1875—78

## To an Unidentified Correspondent[1]

MS. Hyde

[? 1876]                                   *Magdalen College, Oxford*

Thanks. I agree with you about my last verse, but not on your grounds. I don't think the words are beautiful enough for the thought. I think of these three, subject to your decision:

> And yet what changes time can bring!
> The cycles of revolving years
> May free my heart from all it fears
> And teach my { tongue / lips } a song to sing.
>
> Before yon field of { troubled / ruined } gold
> Is garnered into yellow sheaves
> Or ere the autumn's scarlet leaves
> Flutter like birds a-down the wold,
>
> I may have won the better race
> And set my fingers on the goal,
> And looking through the Aureole
> Beheld the Father face to face.
>
> My limbs are overfaint to win
> Or pass beyond the sacred gate,
> Sleep, sleep, O troubled soul and wait
> Till God's own hand shall lead thee in.[2]

I think that would wind it up better. What do you say?
Yours ever                                           OSCAR

[1] Possibly the Irish poet and critic Aubrey De Vere (1814–1902), who was helping Wilde to get his poems published (see *Letters*, p. 26).
[2] The first three of these stanzas, revised and with the third stanza entirely different, were published as Section V of "Graffiti D'Italia" in the September 1876 issue of the *Month and Catholic Review* and, with almost no further changes, as Section IV of "Rome Unvisited" in Wilde's *Poems* (1881).

23

# George Macmillan[1] to his father

MS.   Macmillan

*28 March 1877*                                                    *Genoa*

You will have seen from postcards that we have got so far safely. I am enjoying the trip immensely, though of course the best is to come. As companions form no unimportant element in a journey, I will begin by a word or two on mine. Mahaffy you know.[2] He is most amusing and interesting, and I like him better the more I see of him.

The next man to be mentioned is this young Goulding[3] who you all abused so, but who turns out to be a right good fellow in his way — very full of spirits — delightfully innocent of what we call culture, but still thoroughly entering into the delight of what we see — whether scenery, pictures, palaces etc. In fact he is a downright honest wild Irishman, with no end of fun in him and no particular harm — quite an entertaining companion, and a very good contrast to the last man of the party — for we are four.

This last, who joined us at Charing Cross just as we were starting, is an old pupil of Mahaffy's, and a scholar of Magdalen, Oxford, by name Oscar Wilde. He is a very nice fellow, whose line lies as decidedly in the direction of culture as Goulding's lies away from it. He is aesthetic to the last degree, passionately fond of secondary colours, low tones, Morris papers, and capable of talking a good deal of nonsense thereupon, but for all that a very sensible, well-

---

[1] 1855–1936. Son of Alexander Macmillan, one of the two founding brothers of the publishing firm, which he joined on leaving Eton in 1874. He was made a partner in 1879, and had a great deal to do with the publication of Sir George Grove's *Dictionary of Music* (1878–89) and Sir James Frazer's *The Golden Bough* (1890).

[2] The Rev John Pentland Mahaffy (1839–1919), Professor of Ancient History at Trinity College, Dublin. Knighted 1918.

[3] William Joshua Goulding (1856–1925), son of a wealthy Irish financier.

informed and charming man. Being very impressionable he is just now rather fascinated by Roman Catholicism, and is indeed on his way to Rome, in order to see all the glories of the religion which seems to him the highest and the most sentimental. Mahaffy is quite determined to prevent this if possible, and is using every argument he can to check him. At first he tried hard to persuade him to come to Greece with us, pointing out to him by the way all the worst faults of Popery. Finding this not altogether effective, though it had some weight, he changed his tack, and when Wilde began to say that perhaps he would come, Mahaffy said "I won't take you. I wouldn't have such a fellow with me," which of course, as Wilde is somewhat of a wilful disposition, has raised in him a firm determination to come, and I quite expect he will, and hope so.[1]

Perhaps this is enough about my fellow-travellers, but I assure you I find them endlessly entertaining. Three men more entirely different you could hardly conceive, yet we all get on capitally. Both these fellows are very fond of Mahaffy, though they tell me his unpopularity in Ireland, and in Trinity College Dublin especially, is something remarkable.[2]

## To Keningale Cook[3]
MS. Clark

[c. 20 June 1877]          1 Merrion Square N. [Dublin]

Dear Sir, I am glad to hear from Lady Wilde that you have made the corrections and additions I desired.

[1] Wilde went on to Greece with the others, and they all visited Rome on their way home.
[2] He had been formally censured by the Board of Trinity for abandoning his teaching obligations in favour of a previous journey to Greece. In Ireland generally his noisy contempt for Irish nationalism found little favour.
[3] Keningale Robert Cook (1846–86), Irish poet and writer, editor of the Dublin University Magazine. See Letters, p. 39 and Mason, pp. 67–8.

I think if you had a small notice printed of the contents of the magazine, you would, in Ireland at any rate, increase your sale very much. At present one sees the *D.U.M.* on no bookseller's counter as far as I see in Dublin (except of course your agents'), and how are people to order it if they don't know what they are to get?

I see the *Nineteenth Century* has a full list each month of its articles and contributors, which is put in the windows and on the counters of the booksellers. In Ireland of course any article by my mother is eagerly bought up, but lots of people never hear of them till long after. Wishing you every success, I remain yours truly OSCAR WILDE

## To the Vice-Chancellor of Oxford University
MS. Bodleian

*Monday* [*26 November 1877*]    *Magdalen College, Oxford*

Dear Sir, I desire to have the enclosed bill taxed, as I consider it a most extortionate and exorbitant claim.

The balance of the bill for which this tradesman summoned me was, I think, £5.10: certainly a good deal under six, and it appears to me that if nearly £3 costs are allowed on a £5 bill, the Vice-Chancellory Court must be conducted on a system which requires the investigation of the University Commission.

I trust that this monstrous claim will not be allowed, and remain your obedient servant OSCAR WILDE[1]

---

[1] The tradesman's bill (which is dated 1876) is from G.H. Osmond, jeweller and silversmith of 118 St Aldate's and reads as follows:

| | | |
|---|---|---|
| Set of 18 carat Gold Studs | £2 2 | 0 |
| Gold collar stud | 15 | 0 |
| Ivory ,, ,, | 1 | 0 |
| Rose Croix Apron & Collar | 6 6 | 0 |
| ,, ,, Jewel | 2 5 | 0 |

26

| | | | | |
|---|---|---|---|---|
| ,, ,, Sword & belt | | 2 | 8 | 0 |
| ,, ,, Sword sling 5/- Collaretto 4/- | | | 9 | 0 |
| Case 2/6 Lettering jewel case 1/- | | | 3 | 6 |
| Masonic leather case | | 1 | 8 | 0 |
| Lettering ,, ,, | | | 1 | 0 |
| | | 15 | 18 | 6 |
| Oct 1877 Cash on a/c | | 10 | 0 | 0 |
| | | 5 | 18 | 6 |

All these items had been bought in November 1876, when Wilde had been admitted to the thirty-third degree of the Scottish Masonic rite at the Oxford University chapter, and the bill had been unpaid for almost a year. It was about the court costs that Wilde was complaining.

# LONDON I

## 1879-81

## To George Macmillan
MS. Macmillan

*22 March 1879*                    *St Stephen's Club, Westminster*

Dear Macmillan, I was very glad to get your note and to see that the Society is really to be set on foot: I have every confidence in its success.[1]

Nothing would please me more than to engage in literary work for your House. I have looked forward to this opportunity for some time.

Herodotos I should like to translate very much indeed — selections from that is — and I feel sure that the wonderful picturesqueness of his writings, as well as the pathos and tenderness of some of his stories, would command a great many readers. It is a work I should enjoy doing and should engage to have it done by September 1st next.

I do not know how many Greek plays you intend publishing, but I have been working at Euripides a good deal lately and should of all things wish to edit either the *Mad Hercules* or the *Phoenissae*: plays with which I am well acquainted. I think I see what style of editing is required completely.

I shall be glad to hear from you soon, as well as to see you at Salisbury Street any time you are not busy. Believe me very truly yours                    OSCAR WILDE[2]

## To an Unidentified Correspondent
MS. Hyde

*[Date of receipt 5 November 1879]*        *St Stephen's Club*

Sir, the extremely unsettled state of Ireland, and the im-

[1] Macmillan was one of the founders of the Hellenic Society in 1879.
[2] Macmillan answered on 24 March, welcoming Wilde's suggestions and offering him half-profits with an advance of £25 or £30 for Herodotus, and half-profits or £45 down for the plays. There the matter apparently ended.

possibility of getting rents even after the twenty-five per cent reduction, render it really out of my power to settle your bill. I hope however to do so before the end of the year. Your obedient servant                                    OSCAR WILDE[1]


## To E.F.S. Pigott[2]
MS. Taylor

[*September 1880*]                                    *Keats House, Tite Street*

Dear Mr Pigott, I send you a copy of my first play,[3] which you kindly said you would like to see. Its literary merit is very slight, but in an acting age perhaps the best test of a good play is that it should not read well.

I know only too well how difficult it is to write a really fine drama, but I am working at dramatic art because it's *the democratic* art, and I want fame, so any suggestion, any helpful advice, your experience and very brilliant critical powers can give me I shall thank you very much for.

I think the second act is good writing, and the fourth good position — but how hard to know the value of one's own work! Believe me truly yours                                    OSCAR WILDE


[1] A note on the letter in another hand says the amount owing, which had been outstanding for two years, was £19. 15. 8.
[2] 1826–95. Examiner of Plays for the Lord Chamberlain from 1875. In 1892 he banned Wilde's *Salome*. After his death Bernard Shaw described him as "a walking compendium of vulgar insular prejudice".
[3] The first, privately printed, edition of *Vera; or, The Nihilists* (1880). Wilde's blarney here must have been in hopes of a licence for general production. A proposed morning performance at the Adelphi Theatre, London, with Mrs Bernard Beere in the leading part, was cancelled, and the play was first produced in New York on 11 August 1883, but ran for only a week.

## To Mrs Alfred Hunt[1]

MS. Hyde

[*Postmark 18 November 1880*]                    *Keats House*

Dear Mrs Hunt, I shall be so glad to spend Sunday evening
with you. Will you give Miss Violet the enclosed sonnet. I
promised I would send her my first *political* poem.[2] I should
like to know how far Mr Hunt will agree in my division of
Anarchy from Freedom. Perhaps we shall have a fight over
it on Sunday!

As for Miss Violet, I feel that politics are too harsh an
atmosphere for her: it is like talking to a daffodil about
Political Economy! Still perhaps she may like the form and
the quality, and then I shall be quite happy.

Believe me truly yours                    OSCAR WILDE


## To Rennell Rodd[3]

MS. Private

[*c. 4 December 1880*]                    *Keats House*

Dear Rennell, My best congratulations. Greats is the only
fine school at Oxford, the only sphere of thought where one
can be, *simultaneously*, brilliant and unreasonable, specu-
lative and well-informed, creative as well as critical, and
write with all the passion of youth about the truths which
belong to the august serenity of old age.

I wish you had got a First, that my compeers should not

---

[1] Voluminous novelist (1831–1912). Her daughter Violet was also very
prolific.
[2] "*Libertatis Sacra Fames*," which was published in the *World* on 10
November 1880.
[3] Poet and diplomat (1858–1941). Ambassador to Italy 1908–19.
Created Lord Rennell of Rodd 1933. His Second in Greats was announced in *The Times* on 4 December 1880.

*all* be sluggish and syllogistic Scotchmen; still, a Second is perhaps for a man of culture a sweeter atmosphere than the chilly Caucasus of an atheistical First.

Come back very soon. Truly yours          OSCAR WILDE

## To Clement Scott[1]
MS. Montague

[*20 December 1880*]                                        *Keats House*

Dear Mr Clement Scott, I don't know if you are the author of that charming critique of the *Agamemnon* in the *Telegraph*, but if you are "Clytaemnestra" and "Cassandra" would like to meet you so much and thank you for it.[2]

They and some friends are coming to tea at 5 o'clock tomorrow. If you would join us I should be so pleased.

Very truly yours          OSCAR WILDE

## To Clement Scott
MS. Montague

[*c. 24 December 1880*]                                        *Keats House*

Dear Mr Clement Scott, The price of my poem in your annual is five guineas.[3] I was so sorry, and so were the young Greeks, not to see you on Tuesday. Very truly yours

OSCAR WILDE

[1] 1841–1904. Dramatic critic of the *Daily Telegraph* from 1872 until shortly before his death.

[2] Three performances of the *Agamemnon* of Aeschylus were given by Oxford undergraduates in the St George's Hall, London, on 16, 17 and 18 December 1880. Clytaemnestra was played by F.R. Benson (later Shakespearean actor-manager. 1858–1939. Knighted 1919), and Cassandra by George Lawrence. W.L. Courtney (see note p. 96) was the Watchman.

[3] Wilde's poem "Sen Artysty" appeared in the 1880 edition of Routledge's Christmas Annual *The Green Room*, edited by Clement Scott, and was reprinted in Wilde's *Poems* (1881).

## To George Grossmith[1]

MS. Morgan

*[April 1881]*            *Keats House*

Dear Grossmith, I should like to go to the first night of your new opera at Easter, and would be very much obliged if you would ask the box office to reserve a three-guinea box for me, if there is one to be had: on hearing from the office I will forward a cheque for it.

    With Gilbert and Sullivan I am sure we will have something better than the dull farce of *The Colonel*.[2] I am looking forward to being greatly amused. Very truly yours

OSCAR WILDE


## *Swinburne to Wilde*[3]

*23 July 1881*          *The Pines, Putney Hill*

I am much obliged for the present of your exquisitely pretty book.[4] My time for the present is much taken up with studies of another sort, which claim, as long as they last, a somewhat exclusive devotion: but not so much as to prevent my

---

[1] English comedian and singer (1847–1912). Joint author with his brother Weedon of *The Diary of a Nobody* (1892). On 23 April 1881 at the Opera Comique he created the part of the aesthetic poet Bunthorne in Gilbert and Sullivan's *Patience*. This character was generally taken to be a caricature of Wilde, and the American production of the opera in September was the cause of Wilde's American tour in 1882.

[2] *The Colonel*, a three-act comedy by F.C. Burnand, based on *Le Mari à la campagne*, opened at the Prince of Wales Theatre on 2 February 1881. The character in it called Lambert Streyke was thought to be a caricature of Wilde.

[3] Text from Christie's (New York) catalogue, 6 February 1981.

[4] Wilde's recently published *Poems*.

enjoying such an "impression" (to take the first instance which occurs to me) as that at p. 143.[1]

A. C. SWINBURNE

## To the Librarian of the Oxford Union Society[2]

*[Early November 1881] 9 Charles Street, Grosvenor Square*[3]

Dear Sir, Pray assure the committee of the Oxford Union that, while regretting that they had not ascertained the feeling of the Society with regard to my art, I quite acquit them of any intention to be discourteous towards me, and that I readily accept an apology so sincerely offered.

My chief regret indeed being that there should still be at Oxford such a large number of young men who are ready to accept their own ignorance as an index, and their own conceit as a criterion of any imaginative and beautiful work. I must also, for the sake of the good fame and position of the Oxford Union, express a hope that no other poet or writer of

[1] LES SILHOUETTES

The sea is flecked with bars of grey,
The dull dead wind is out of tune,
And like a withered leaf the moon
Is blown across the stormy bay.

Etched clear upon the pallid sand
Lies the black boat: a sailor boy
Clambers aboard in careless joy
With laughing face and gleaming hand.

And overhead the curlews cry,
Where through the dusky upland grass
The young brown-throated reapers pass,
Like silhouettes against the sky.

[2] The librarian of the Oxford Union had asked Wilde for a copy of his *Poems*, and Wilde had sent an inscribed copy. At a meeting of the Union on 3 November 1881 a proposal to accept this gift was defeated by 140 votes to 128. Text from the *Autograph*, Vol I, No 2, December 1911.
[3] From this and the following letter it seems clear that Wilde stayed at this address for a few weeks before he left for America on 24 December.

English will ever be subjected to what I feel sure you as well as myself are conscious of, the coarse impertinence of having a work officially rejected which has been no less officially sought for.

Pray be kind enough to forward to my private address the volume of my poems,[1] and believe me, yours truly

OSCAR WILDE

## To the Hon. George Curzon[2]
MS. Curzon

[*November 1881*[3]]                    *9 Charles Street*

My dear Curzon, You are a brick! and I thank you very much for your chivalrous defence of me in the Union. So much of what is best in England passes through Oxford that I should have been sorry to think that discourtesy so gross and narrow-mindedness so evil could have been suffered to exist without some voice of scorn being raised against them.[4]

Our sweet city with its dreaming towers must not be given entirely over to the Philistines. They have Gath and Ekron and Ashdod and many other cities of dirt and dread and despair, and we must not yield them the quiet cloister of Magdalen to brawl in, or the windows of Merton to peer from.

I hope you will come and see me in town. I have left my house at Chelsea but will be always delighted to see you, for,

[1] Now in the Hyde collection.
[2] Oxford friend of Wilde (1859–1925), son of Lord Scarsdale. Later M.P. Baron 1898, Viceroy of India 1898–1905, Foreign Secretary 1919–24, Marquess 1921.
[3] So dated by recipient.
[4] It was in the Union debate of 17 November that Curzon attacked the Union's treatment of Wilde's *Poems*.

in spite of the story of Aristides,[1] I have not got tired yet of hearing Rennell Rodd call you perfect.

I send you a bill of my first attack on Tyranny.[2] I wish you could get it posted in the "High", but perhaps I bother you? Very truly yours                                          OSCAR WILDE

[1] Athenian general and archon (?530–468 B.C.). He supposedly voted for his own ostracism on hearing a voter declare against him because he was tired of Aristides being called "The Just".
[2] Probably announcing the performance of *Vera*, which was planned for 17 December 1881, but later cancelled.

# AMERICA

1882

## To Mrs George Lewis[1]

MS. Rosenbach

[17 January 1882[2]]                                        *Philadelphia*

My dear Mrs Lewis, Everything is going on brilliantly. I send you papers regularly. Of course they are full of lies, but you will not take them seriously. I go to see Walt Whitman, at his invitation, tomorrow. Tonight I lecture to 1500 people. Best regards to Mr Lewis and Mr Burne-Jones.[3] Truly yours

OSCAR WILDE


## To Charles Eliot Norton[4]

MS. Taylor

[c. 28 January 1882]                                *Vendome Hotel, Boston*

Dear Professor Norton, I am in Boston for a few days, and hope you will allow me the pleasure of calling on you. I cannot tell you how I look forward to meeting one of whom Edward Burne-Jones so constantly and so affectionately is talking. I remain most truly yours        OSCAR WILDE

---

[1] Betty Eberstadt (1844–1931), wife of George Lewis (1833–1911), the most successful solicitor of his time. He was knighted in 1893 and made Baronet in 1902.
[2] When Wilde lectured in the Horticultural Hall at Philadelphia.
[3] Edward Burne-Jones, painter (1833–98). Made a Baronet 1894.
[4] American scholar and man of letters (1827–1908). Friend of Longfellow, Emerson, Carlyle, Ruskin, FitzGerald and Henry James. For Burne-Jones's letter of introduction see *Letters*, p. 123.

## To Colonel W.F. Morse[1]
### MS. Montague

*[?. c 12 February 1882]*        *Grand Pacific Hotel, Chicago*

Dear Colonel Morse, I hope you will arrange some more matinées: *to lecture does not tire me.* I would sooner lecture five or six times a week, and travel only three or four hours a day, than lecture three times and travel ten hours. I do not think I should ever lecture less than four times, and these matinées are a great hit. Let me know what we are to do after Cincinnati — is it Canada? I am ready to lecture till last week in April — *April 25th,* say. Yours truly

OSCAR WILDE


## To the Hon. George Curzon
### MS. Curzon

*15 February 1882*                                          *U.S.*

My dear George Curzon, Yes! You are on the black list, and, if my secretary does his work properly, every mail shall hurl at your young philosophic head the rage of the American eagle because I do not think trousers beautiful, the excitement of a sane strong people over the colour of my necktie, the fear of the eagle that I have come to cut his barbaric claws with the scissors of culture, the impotent rage of the ink-stained, the noble and glorious homage of the respectable — you shall know it all: it may serve you for marginal notes περὶ δημοκρατίας.[2]

Well, it's really wonderful, my audiences are enormous. In Chicago I lectured last Monday to 2500 people! This is of

---

[1] The American representative of Richard D'Oyly Carte (see note p. 44). This letter appeared in an abbreviated and inaccurate form in *Letters.*
[2] Concerning democracy.

course nothing to anyone who has spoken at the Union, but to me it was delightful — a great sympathetic electric people, who cheered and applauded and gave me a sense of serene power that even being abused by the *Saturday Review* never gave me.[1]

I lecture four times a week, and the people are delightful and lionize one to a curious extent, but they follow me, and start schools of design when I visit their town. At Philadelphia the school is called after me and they really are beginning to love and know beautiful art and its meaning.

As for myself, I feel like Tancred or Lothair.[2] I travel in such state, for in a *free* country one cannot live without slaves, and I have slaves — black, yellow and white. But you must write again. Your letter had a flavour of Attic salt.

Yours (from Boeotia[3]) OSCAR WILDE

## To Mrs Bernard Beere[4]

[*? c. 20 March 1882*] [*? Sioux City*]

I don't know where I am, but I am among cañons and coyotes: one is a sort of fox, the other a deep ravine: I don't know which is which, but it does not really matter in the West ... I have also seen Indians: most of them are curiously

---

[1] The *Saturday Review* notice of Wilde's *Poems* on 23 July 1881 ended: "The book is not without traces of cleverness, but is marred everywhere by imitation, insincerity, and bad taste."

[2] The eponymous heroes of Disraeli's novels, both adventurous young men. On a later occasion (*Letters*, p. 178) Wilde compared Curzon to the young Coningsby. Clearly Disraeli's novels were a shared interest.

[3] A province of Greece proverbial for the dullness and stupidity of its inhabitants.

[4] English actress (1856–1915). The text of this fragment is taken from Sotheby's catalogue–3 December 1915.

like Joe Knight[1] in appearance, a few are like Alfred Thompson,[2] and when on the war trail they look like a *procession of Salas*.[3] . . . I've also met miners who are nearly as real as Bret Harte,[4] and I have lectured, and raced, and been lionised, and adored, and assailed, and mocked at, and worshipped, but of course as usual quite triumphant.

## To Richard D'Oyly Carte[5]

MS. Private

[*c. March 1882*]

Dear Mr Carte, I think if some large lithographs of me were got it would help business in these small cities, where the local men spend so little on advertising.

The photograph of me with head looking over my shoulder would be the best — just the head and fur collar. Will you see to this? Also, please tell Miss Morris[6] that the novel *The Nihilist Princess* is a sham, and empty of all dramatic matter. She had been afraid of it. Yours truly

OSCAR WILDE

[1] English dramatic critic (1829–1907).
[2] Dramatic author and designer (died 1895).
[3] George Augustus Sala, flamboyant journalist and novelist (1828–95).
[4] American writer and poet of the wild west (1836–1902), whom Wilde described as "a lord of romance".
[5] Impresario (1844–1901) who produced many of the Gilbert and Sullivan operas and promoted Wilde's American tour.
[6] Clara Morris, American actress (1848–1925), who Wilde hoped would play the leading part in *Vera; or, The Nihilists*.

## To Mrs Blakeney[1]

MS. Morgan

[c. 2 April 1882]                    The Palace Hotel, San Francisco

Dear Mrs Blakeney, I thank you very much for the photograph of May, which will remind me always of the prettiest child I have seen in America. She is like a wonderful little flower, and if flowers could talk so sweetly as she does who would not be a gardener! She is quite bird-like in her lightness and poise, and I hope she will not ever fly away.

I have sent to every place in San Francisco for a photograph of myself, and hope to get one by tomorrow and will bring it to Sacramento on Saturday, when I will look forward to the pleasure of giving it to you in person. In fact I have an irresistible presentiment that I will see you.

Pray give my love to May, and believe me most truly yours                                                    OSCAR WILDE


## To J.M. Stoddart[2]

MS. Montague

17 April [1882]                              Kansas City [Missouri]

Dear Mr Stoddart, I send you the proof.[3] There are a good many corrections, so perhaps I had better have another, to

---

[1] Mrs Mary Miller Blakeney was President of the Women's Literary Club in Sacramento, where Wilde had lectured on 31 March. May was her ten-year-old daughter. Wilde lectured again at Sacramento on Saturday, 8 April, and afterwards dined with the Blakeneys.
[2] Philadelphia publisher (1845–1921).
[3] Of *Rose Leaf and Apple Leaf* by Rennell Rodd, which was substantially a new edition of Rodd's *Songs in the South* (1881), with an introduction (envoi) by Wilde and a dedication to himself. These two additions annoyed Rodd. Stoddart published the book later in 1882.

45

see that it is all right — especially the *French*. * You might yourself see that the accents etc are right. I'm working east now, so the proof could be returned immediately. *Yes*: I must have a final proof — as soon as possible. Yours truly

OSCAR WILDE

Yes: include the poem I sent you — *before* "Tiber Mouth". Also send me a proof of it. I should mention it in the preface. I am sorry you've been ill.
Where is Whitman? In Camden town?[1]

* Such as *Pour moi je préfère les poètes qui font des vers, les médecins qui sachent guérir, les peintres qui sachent peindre.*


## To Colonel W.F. Morse
TS. Clark

*17 April [1882]*                                    *Kansas City*

I have received a good offer for two months' light lecturing in the South which I am anxious to visit. Send me a wire to say what you think of my accepting it.

I will send the deed for the clothes. Would you order for me, from some one who understands costume, a cambric shirt, suitable for dress of last century. At Mrs Crosby's[2] I will appear in a new departure in evening dress, black velvet with lace.


[1] Walt Whitman lived in Camden, New Jersey.
[2] Jennie M. Wolcott married (1880) George Harrington Crosby, an American railway financier (died 1927).

46

## To Julia Ward Howe[1]

[*14 July 1882*[2]]                    [*Newport, Rhode Island*]

Dear Mrs Howe, I shall be with you at seven o'clock, but there is no such thing as dining with *you en famille*. When you are present, the air is cosmopolitan and the room seems to be full of brilliant people. You are one of those rare persons who give one the sense of creating history as they live.

No, *en famille* is impossible, but to dine with you one of the great privileges. Most truly yours     OSCAR WILDE


## To John Boyle O'Reilly[3]
### MS. Texas

[*27 September 1882*]
                    *The Pilot, 597 Washington Street, Boston*

My dear Boyle, Why are you out? Dining too, which aggravates it. I want to see you about my mother's poems. I think your idea of a preface is excellent.

She is very anxious to have them brought out, and if you

---

[1] American author and reformer (1819–1910), author of "The Battle Hymn of the Republic" (1861). See *Letters*, p. 122.
[2] Wilde and Sam Ward, Mrs Howe's brother, arrived at Newport on 13 July, dined with Mrs Howe next day, and spent the night at her house. Wilde lectured at the Casino in Newport on 15 July. Text and information from *This Was My Newport* (1944) by Mrs Howe's daughter Maude Howe Elliott (1854–1948).
[3] 1844–90. He had in 1868 been transported from Ireland to Australia for Fenian activities. He escaped to the United States in 1870, became an American citizen and devoted himself to journalism. As editor and part-proprietor of the *Boston Pilot* he did much for the cause of Irish Nationalism and encouraged many young Irish writers. He was the first person to publish a poem of Wilde's in America.

will induce Roberts[1] to do it she will send you her later work, which is so strong and splendid.

I lecture tonight at Lynn,[2] and may be passing through Boston tomorrow. If I knew your hours I would come and see you, but I can't if you insist on taking dinner at the wrong time.

I think my mother's work should make a great success here: it is so unlike the work of her degenerate artistic son. I know you think I am thrilled by nothing but a dado.[3] You are quite wrong, but I shan't argue. Ever yours

OSCAR WILDE

## To Samuel Ward[4]

MS. Montague

[c. 24 October 1882]          85 Clinton Place, New York

My dear Uncle Sam, The Lily[5] is very anxious to see you: suppose that we have a *lunch* on Sunday — *not a dinner* — for her. But of course she will be here five weeks. There is lots of time.

I come back *Friday* morning. Ever yours          OSCAR

---

[1] One of the Roberts Brothers, Boston publishers, who brought out the authorised American editions of Wilde's *Poems* (1881) and *The Happy Prince* (1888).

[2] A manufacturing city and seaport, nine miles north-east of Boston. Wilde lectured in the Music Hall there on Decorative Art in America on 27 September.

[3] A skirting of wood along the lower part of the walls of a room.

[4] American lobbyist, financier, talker and gastronome (1814–84). Described by Lord Rosebery as "the uncle of the human race".

[5] Lily Langtry (1852–1929), famous beauty and close friend of the Prince of Wales, had recently started acting professionally, and had just arrived in New York for her theatrical début there.

## To Mrs Bigelow[1]
### MS. NYPL

[*Late October 1882*]                    [*New York*]

Dear Mrs Bigelow, Mrs Langtry is hard at work at rehearsals
all day long, but will be at home at five o'clock *I think*, and
will be charmed I feel sure to have the pleasure of receiving
a visit from you. I hope you will do her the honour of calling
— with the accompanying note from me. As for Sunday
night I will be very pleased indeed to come. Ever yours

                                        OSCAR WILDE


## To Henry Edwards[2]
### MS. Hyde

[*? Late October 1882*]        *48 West 11* [*New York City*]

Dear Mr Edwards, I am anxious to ask you about Australia,
and my trip there, and under whose management I should
go. Will you be at the Lambs[3] tonight after the play? If not
would you send a line there to let me know. Very truly yours

                                        OSCAR WILDE


[1] Wife of John Bigelow (1817–1911), American diplomat, author and
editor. A few days after Wilde's arrival in America Mr and Mrs Bigelow
entertained him at dinner in their house at 21 Gramercy Park.
[2] American actor and scientist (1830–91). This letter is addressed to him
at Wallack's Theatre, where he was acting in G.W. Godfrey's *The
Parvenu*.
[3] A New York theatrical club.

# To Mrs Dion Boucicault[1]

[*31 October 1882*]                                      *New York*

I cannot get anything for Salvini tomorrow night, but hope that before he closes I may have the pleasure of seeing him with you.[2]

Poor Mrs Langtry is dreadfully upset by the catastrophe; she had only left the theatre a few hours.[3]

---

[1] Agnes Kelly Robertson (1833–1916), actress and common-law wife of Dionysius Lardner Boucicault, Irish dramatist and actor (1820–90). Text from the *Autograph*, Vol 1, No 5, May 1912.

[2] Tommaso Salvini, leading Italian actor (1830–1915). His last evening performance of *Othello* in this season was on 1 November. He spoke in Italian, the rest of the cast in English.

[3] On 30 October, the day before what should have been Mrs Langtry's first night, the Park Theatre was burnt to the ground. She opened six days later, on 6 November, at Wallack's Theatre in *An Unequal Match* by Tom Taylor. Wilde's enthusiastic review, extolling Mrs Langtry's beauty and clothes, but tactfully refraining from mention of the play itself, appeared in the *New York World* on 7 November. It was reprinted in *Miscellanies*. Boucicault had introduced the fire-proofing of theatrical scenery to Wallack's Theatre in 1876.

# LONDON II

1883-90

## To Théodore Duret[1]

MS. Dallas

[*April 1883*]                                    Hôtel Voltaire [*Paris*]

Cher Monsieur Duret, Je serai tout à fait charmé d'avoir le plaisir de visiter Monsieur de Goncourt[2] avec vous mercredi prochain: il est, pour moi, un des plus grands maîtres de la prose moderne, et son roman de *Manette Salomon* est un chef d'oeuvre.

Je vous remercie bien de votre courtoisie, et de votre introduction à M. Zola, de laquelle je ne manquerai pas de me profiter.

Acceptez l'assurance de mes sentiments les plus distingués.                                    OSCAR WILDE


## To the Royal Academy Students

MS. Kaufmann

[*Postmark 2 June 1883*]                                    [*London*]

Gentlemen, I have the pleasure of accepting the courteous invitation of your club to lecture before it on Saturday evening June 30 at 8.30 o'clock.

I remain, Gentlemen, your obedient servant
                                                   OSCAR WILDE[3]


[1] French author and art-critic (1838–1927).
[2] Edmond de Goncourt, French diarist, novelist, historian and collector (1822–96).
[3] The arrangements for this lecture were made by, and this acceptance was sent to, Wilde's friend Eric Forbes-Robertson, who was a student at the R.A. In a brief note to him Wilde wrote: "I should like it to be confined to the students entirely, and a *student* in the chair." The lecture was delivered on 30 June at the students' club in Golden Square. It was printed, from the manuscript, in *Miscellanies*.

## To Mrs Millais[1]

MS. Hyde

[*c. 3 June 1883*]     *9 Charles Street, Grosvenor Square*

Dear Mrs Millais, Here are the Lily's views on American women.[2] Very sweetly expressed, I think they are, and a lesson in courtesy to a nation which has been discourteous to her.[3] I hope they will interest you. They are really very clever, but then all beautiful women are more or less verbally inspired. Believe me most truly yours  OSCAR WILDE

## To Eric Forbes-Robertson

MS. Kaufmann

[*Early July 1883*]

My dear Eric, In case you and any of your brother students care to be lectured a second time on not so charming a subject as art I send you six tickets for yourself and them.[4] Truly yours                        OSCAR WILDE

---

[1] Euphemia (Effie) Gray (1829–97) married (1855) John Everett Millais, the painter (1829–96), after the annulment of her marriage to John Ruskin.

[2] A long article in a supplement of the *New York Times*.

[3] The American press had belittled her acting and made much of her love-life.

[4] For Wilde's lecture on "Personal Impressions of America" at the Princes' Hall, Piccadilly, on Tuesday 10 July 1883.

# To Harry Nash[1]

*Saturday evening [3 November 1883]*
*Newlyn's Family Hotel, Bournemouth*

Dear Mr Nash, I am very sorry that through an oversight on the part of my secretary I was led to suppose that my lecture was fixed for to-night instead of this afternoon — a mistake which I have only discovered on my arrival here this evening. I cannot sufficiently regret that I have been deprived of the privilege of lecturing before a Bournemouth audience; and beg that you will convey to the public my sincere apology for this unintentional discourtesy, and accept yourself my regrets for the trouble you have been caused. I hope that some day I will have the opportunity of speaking in your theatre; that is to say if I am ever forgiven in Bournemouth.[2] I remain yours truly      OSCAR WILDE

[1] A "large and fashionable" audience had assembled at the Theatre Royal, Bournemouth, on the afternoon of Saturday 3 November in anticipation of a lecture by Wilde on "The House Beautiful". Wilde did not arrive and the audience were persuaded by the Manager, Mr Harry Nash, to wait for half an hour in case Wilde had missed an earlier train from Exeter (where he had lectured the previous evening). He was not on the next train, and the audience were given their money back. The Manager published Wilde's letter of explanation and apology in *The Bournemouth Observer and Visitors' List* of 7 November 1883, from which this text is taken. Harry Nash was also a "General Advertising Agent and Bill Poster" and partner in a firm of printers and stationers.

[2] He was: he gave highly successful lectures on the following Friday evening and Saturday afternoon (9 and 10 November) on "Personal Impressions of America" and "The House Beautiful".

## To G.W. Appleton[1]
### MS. Private

*[c. 22 February* 1884][2]    *County Hotel, Ulverston, Lancs*

Dear Mr Appleton, *Why* do I see Greenock: "Value of Art in Modern Life"? I am tired of telling you I will not deliver that lecture except when I give two lectures in the same town, and on different days. Nothing puts me out so much as these things which are constantly occurring.

Of course it will mean a row with the Society. I am getting sick of the whole thing. Yours truly          O.W.


## To G.W. Appleton
### MS. Koch

*[c. March 1884]*                        *16 Tite Street*

Dear Mr Appleton, The lecture cannot be on Cellini — it is on Dress. I hope there is no mull in the matter.

Will you kindly let me have the American and English books of criticisms. I want to arrange a collection. I should like them this week. Truly yours          OSCAR WILDE


## To the Editor of the Pall Mall Gazette
### MS. Private

*[c. 11 November 1884]*    *Great Western Hotel, Birmingham*
*Private*

Dear Sir, There are a few printer's errors in my article on Dress, which, if you think of including it in the *Budget,* I

---

[1] 1845–1909. The London organiser of Wilde's British lecture-tour.
[2] On that day Wilde lectured on "The House Beautiful" to the Ulverston Literary Society in the Temperance Hall, Ulverston.

would like to have corrected, as per enclosed.[1] I hardly know if I might ask you to have the drawing I sent you printed on a portion of the paper that has *no printing on the other side*: it does so ruin the delicacy and artistic value of the block: perhaps however this is asking too much. I remain, sir, your obedient servant                                    OSCAR WILDE

I find that some confusion as to the two drawings has been caused, so I have put a ? after Mr Huyshe's "Ideal Dress" simply to show it is not my idea.


## To Mrs H.C. Merivale[2]

MS. Hyde

[*? Early 1885*]                                    *Queens Hotel, Eastbourne*

My dear Mrs Merivale, The weather has so disappointed me here that I am going back to town this afternoon, and will have to give up your very charming invitation to dine with you. I hope to have the pleasure of calling on you when you are at Lady Collier's:[3] we will be close neighbours then. Pray let me know when you are there, and remember me most warmly to your husband: I know no more brilliant talker, no more delightful companion. As for his play, I must write to him about it: it is very beautiful, and grandly powerful.[4] Truly yours                                    OSCAR WILDE


[1] The *Pall Mall Budget* was a weekly collection of articles from the *Pall Mall Gazette*, an evening paper. Wilde's article "More Radical Ideas upon Dress Reform" appeared in the *Gazette* on 11 November 1884 and in the *Budget* on 14 November. It had one illustration by Wentworth Huyshe and one by E.W. Godwin.
[2] Elizabeth (née Pitman), actress wife of Herman Charles Merivale, playwright and novelist (1839–1906). They lived at Eastbourne.
[3] 1815–86. Wife of Sir Robert Collier, barrister and M.P. (1817–86) who was created Lord Monkswell in 1885.
[4] *Florien, A Tragedy in Five Acts*, published in 1884.

## To Lily Langtry
MS. Hyde

[*6 April 1885*][1]                                    [*16 Tite Street*]

Constance's[2] doctor has just been here, and won't hear of
her going out tonight as we dined out yesterday. And I don't
like leaving her: you know she is going to have a child. So I
send back the stalls with many thanks to you, and many
regrets. Perhaps you would let us have two stalls, or a spare
box, on *Wednesday* next, when Constance would like to
come immensely. She is in hopes you will come and have tea
with her some day. She wants to show you her house, which
I think you will like. Ever yours                     OSCAR

I would have taken the liberty of giving the stalls away had
it not been a "*première*", but I know how anxious every-
body is to see your Lady Ormond.


## To H.C. Marillier[3]
MS. Hyde

[*Postmark 14 November 1885*]                     *16 Tite Street*

My dear Harry, The army is a noble profession. I would
sooner see you in a cocked hat than see you a curate, or a
solicitor. A man of brains can always be fine, and I think you
are right to go in for the examination, though I wonder you

[1] When Mrs Langtry opened at the Prince's Theatre, London, in
*Peril*, an adaptation of Sardou's *Nos Intimes*, originally produced in
London in 1876. Mrs Langtry had already played the part of Lady
Ormond in America.
[2] Wilde had married Constance Lloyd on 29 May 1884.
[3] 1865–1951. He had lodged at 13 Salisbury Street, Strand, when Wilde
was living there (1880–81). Now he was a classical scholar at Peterhouse,
Cambridge. Later he became an author and art-critic.

dislike the idea of being a schoolmaster. With your quick sympathies, your delicate intuition, and your enthusiasm, you could teach wonderfully. You have the power of making others love you, which is the first essential of a teacher. For my own part I think the life of a teacher the loveliest in the world. But wherever you are, whatever your profession, you will make a mark and carve a destiny. I felt that when I met you, I know it now that we have written to each other.

I wonder are you all as cold in Cambridge as we are. I love the languor of hot noons, and hate our chill winter — so pitiless, so precise — giving one form where one wants colour, definiteness where one needs mystery, and making poor humanity red-nosed and blue-nosed and horrid. I think I had better not come down to Cambridge. You should be reading and I would idle you. You should dream of parallelograms not of poetry, and only talk of x and y. What do you say? Life is long and we will see each other often. In the meantime we can write. Also, send me a photograph of yourself.

Sayle[1] of New College has sent me his poems. Do you know him? There is one very lovely sonnet. Affectionately yours                                                        OSCAR

## To H.C. Marillier
MS. Hyde

[*Postmark 16 November 1885*]                      *16 Tite Street*

What is Harry doing? Is he reading Shelley in a land of moonbeams and mystery? Or rowing in Babylonish garments on the river? Is the world a dust-heap or a flower-garden to him? Poisonous, or perfect, or both?          O.W.

---

[1] Charles Edward Sayle (1864–1924), who worked for most of his life in Cambridge University Library. His book of poems *Bertha: a Story of Love* was published anonymously in 1885.

# To Gabriel Sarrazin[1]

MS. Pennsylvania

[1885]                                                                 16 Tite Street

My dear Sarrazin, I have delayed answering your letter and thanking you for your delightful book till I had read the latter. You certainly have an exquisite critical insight into the secrets of our poetry, and your articles on Shelley and on Rossetti are admirable.[2]

I hope to send you my own poems next week, and I look forward with much pleasure to being read by so subtle a critic, and so generous an admirer.

Whenever you come to London you will always find a warm welcome waiting for you; you have here many friends, amongst whom I hope to class myself.

My wife sends you her kindest regards, and with many thanks for your charming volume, believe me sincerely yours                                                                 OSCAR WILDE


# To H.C. Marillier

MS. Hyde

[Postmark 1 January 1886]                                         Albemarle Club

Wednesday 4.10 I will come down. Who is Osman?[3]

Let us live like Spartans, but let us talk like Athenians. Ever yours                                                                 OSCAR

[1] French critic (b.1853) who wrote essays on French literature in the *Athenaeum*. He contributed an article on the French novelist Georges Ohnet to the May 1889 issue of the *Woman's World*.
[2] In Sarrazin's *Poètes Modernes en Angleterre* (1885).
[3] Osman Edwards (1864–1936) had been at school with Marillier at Christ's Hospital. At this time he was an Oxford undergraduate. Later he was reviewer, lecturer, translator, amateur of the theatre, and a master at St Paul's School.

# To the Secretary of the Beaumont Trust
## MS. QMC

*Monday, 22 February 1886*                    *16 Tite Street*

Sir, I beg to offer myself as a candidate for the Secretaryship to the Beaumont Trust Fund, an office which I understand will shortly be vacant.

During my university career I obtained two First Classes, the Newdigate Prize, and other honours, and since taking my degree, in 1878, I have devoted myself partly to literature and partly to the spreading of art-knowledge and art-appreciation among the people.

I have had the opportunity in America of studying the various forms of technical education, from the Cooper Institute in New York to Mr Leland's Art-School for Children in Philadelphia, and have constantly lectured on the subject in this country before Art-Schools, Mechanics' Institutes and Literary Societies.

Should the trustees of the Beaumont Scheme consider me worthy to hold the post of Secretary, I would be able to devote all my time to the fulfilment of the necessary duties and the furtherance of the proposed movement, as I have no formal profession but that of literature and art-culture.

This People's Palace will be to me the realization of much that I have long hoped for, and to be in any way officially connected with it would be esteemed by me a high and noble honour.[1] I remain, sir, your obedient servant,

OSCAR WILDE

---

[1] The People's Palace in the Mile End Road was opened by Queen Victoria on 14 May 1887. It was designed "as an institution, in which, whether in Science, Art or Literature, any student may be able to follow up his education to the highest point by means of Technical and Trades Schools, Reading Rooms and Libraries". It is now part of Queen Mary College in the University of London.

## To Sir Edmund Currie[1]
### MS. QMC

*22 February 1886*                                    *16 Tite Street*

Dear Sir Edmund Currie, I have sent in to the Trustees of the Beaumont Trust Fund an application for the post of Secretary.

I am very anxious to be connected officially with the People's Palace, as I have devoted myself entirely to the spreading of art-culture among the people, and have had, both in America and in this country, many opportunities of studying the possibility of a wider technical education than modern systems afford.

My acquaintance with you is so slight that I hardly venture to ask for your personal support, though that would be to me of inestimable value [*The rest of this letter is missing*].


## To Henry E. Dixey[2]
### MS. Koch

*[Early June 1886]*                                    *16 Tite Street*

My dear Adonis, I am delighted to see that, though the critics do not quite like your play, they all recognise the charm and grace of your acting.

For myself, I wish you were a wave of the sea, that you might be always dancing.[3] Every movement and gesture

---

[1] 1834–1913. Chairman of the People's Palace Trustees. Knighted 1876.
[2] American actor (1859–1943). His burlesque *Adonis*, in which he played the title-rôle, opened on 4 September 1884 at the Bijou Theatre, New York, and on 31 May 1886, at the Gaiety Theatre, London, where it ran for three months. In it Dixey gave an imitation of Irving which drew the town. Wilde's brother Willie reviewed *Adonis* in the *Theatre* for 1 July, and Wilde probably saw it early in its run.
[3] Cf. *The Winter's Tale*, Act IV, scene iv.

that you make is instinct with natural beauty, and expressive of the loveliness of mere life.

Some afternoon I will come and sit with you, if you let me, while you are dining.

You have all my best wishes and congratulations. Very truly yours                    OSCAR WILDE

## To H.C. Marillier
### MS. Hyde

[*Postmark 11 June 1886*]

Your letter came to me at Manchester. I had been thinking a great deal about you. There is at least this beautiful mystery in life, that at the moment it feels most complete it finds some secret sacred niche in its shrine empty and waiting.

Then comes a time of exquisite expectancy.

Harry, you must not ask me to read a paper, or say anything. I have too much public work at present and am tired. I shall look and listen, and my visit will be quite quiet. Perhaps next term.

You are certainly not to call me Mr Wilde. What should you call me but                    OSCAR

## To Herbert P. Horne[1]
### MS. Clark

[*Date of receipt 14 July 1886*]                    16 Tite Street

I fear I have to go out tonight, but I hope to see you soon.

Your poems are most charming, and your choice of

---

[1] Architect, connoisseur and art historian (1864–1916). Built the Church of the Redeemer, Bayswater Road. In 1886, with his partner A.H. Mackmurdo, he started a periodical called *The Century Guild Hobby Horse*, in which he printed some of his poems.

epithets exquisite and felicitous. You combine very perfectly simplicity and strangeness. I have no doubt you will do very lovely work.                           OSCAR WILDE


## To E.T. Cook[1]

[c. 23 November 1886]                          Castle Hotel, Windsor

My dear Cook, I was very much pleased with the article. It was exceedingly fair and the whole tone of it right. And I must thank you for holding your reviewer.[2]

I think however that the rule about inverted commas is a little strict. For instance, in Roden Noel's book there occurs this amazing sentence. "I know not any *artist of note*, unless it be Edgar Poe, Bulwer Lytton, Disraeli, or *Mr Alfred Austin* whom we may affiliate on Byron"!!!! I quote it as follows: that Edgar Poe, Disraeli, and Mr Alfred Austin are "artists of note whom we may affiliate on Byron". I have

[1] Edward Tyas Cook (1857–1919) was at this time working on the *Pall Mall Gazette* under W.T. Stead, whom he succeeded as editor in 1890. He was later editor of the *Westminster Gazette* and the *Daily News*. He wrote biographies and, with Alexander Wedderburn, edited the thirty-eight volumes of Ruskin's *Works* (1903–1911). He was knighted in 1912. The text of this letter is taken from the *Serif*, Kent, Ohio, September 1971.

[2] On 18 November 1886 the *Pall Mall Gazette* published Wilde's long and anonymous review of Harry Quilter's *Sententiae Artis*, which he demolished with humour and good sense. On 23 November the paper printed an angry letter from Quilter, in which he attempted to refute Wilde's criticisms. Immediately below this was printed a page-long "editor's note", which, clearly fuelled by Wilde, showed that in every particular Wilde was right and Quilter wrong. This is the "article" in Wilde's letter. In it the editor apologised for the use of inverted commas round phrases that were not the exact words of the writer. For Quilter see note p. 83.

64

removed the inverted commas in my proof, but I think they might have stood.[1]

I have done Skipsey and two other poets for you. You will have the manuscript on Monday.[2] I return to town to-morrow morning.

Have you any more books for me? I suppose Henry James's last novel is done?[3] Very sincerely yours

OSCAR WILDE


## To S. Wall Richards[4]

MS. Clark

[Postmark 16 March 1887]                    16 Tite Street

Dear Mr Wall Richards, I am so sorry, but it is quite impossible. I am too busy to lecture, and the subjects you mention I have already given at Bournemouth. Otherwise I would only be too glad to speak again under your auspices.

Would you kindly tell me what fee I was paid for my lecture this year. Was it £8.8 or £12.12? I want to get my accounts in order for the Income Tax.

I hope you are all well, and remain truly yours

OSCAR WILDE


[1] Wilde's review of Roden Noel's *Essays on Poetry and Poets* appeared in the *Pall Mall Gazette* on 1 December 1886, with the second pair of inverted commas removed. It was reprinted in *Reviews*.

[2] Joseph Skipsey (1832–1903), Northumberland collier-poet. Wilde's review of his *Carols from the Coalfields* appeared in the *Pall Mall Gazette* on 1 February 1887 and was reprinted in *Reviews*.

[3] *The Bostonians* (1886). Wilde reviewed none of Henry James's novels in the *P.M.G.*

[4] He and his wife ran a family boarding house at their home The Grange, West Cliff, Bournemouth. They also ran a series of "weekly entertainments" in the Shaftesbury Hall, Bournemouth. Wilde had lectured there on Dress on 28 January 1887 and spent the night at the Grange.

# To Alsagar Vian[1]

*Monday* [*Postmark 11 April 1887*]                    *Abbots Hill*[2]

Dear Vian, I send you my article on the play, and will be at office tomorrow (12–1.30) to see it right.

Will you see that my paragraph about the Children's Hospital scheme is all right, and that *no other Hospital* paragraph goes in this week. The Prince's daughters are very much interested in it, as I have mentioned. So it shows philanthropy in its relation to Society, which I am told is the keynote of social papers.[3]

Enclosed may amuse you.[4] Truly yours     OSCAR WILDE

We must have an evening together soon over our "Journalism" article.


# To Alsagar Vian[5]

[*Postmark 13 April 1887*]                         *16 Tite Street*

My dear Vian, Shall I do for you an article called "The Child Philosopher"? It will be on Mark Twain's amazing and amusing record of the answers of American children at a Board School.

Some of them such as *Republican* — "a sinner mentioned

---

[1] Editor of the *Court and Society Review*. Father of Admiral of the Fleet Sir Philip Vian. Text from a transcript in an unknown hand.

[2] The house, near Hemel Hempstead in Hertfordshire, of John Dickinson (see *Letters*, p. 220), where Wilde often stayed.

[3] Wilde's paragraph on the Great Ormond Street Hospital and his review of *Held by the Enemy*, a drama in five acts by William Gillette, both appeared in the issue of 13 April 1887. They were reprinted in Mason.

[4] Probably Wilde's article "The American Man", which also appeared in the issue of 13 April.

[5] Text from a transcript in an unknown hand.

in the Bible", or *Democrat* — "a vessel usually filled with beer", are excellent.[1]

Come and dine at *Pagani's* in Portland Street on Friday — 7.30. No dress, just ourselves and a flask of Italian wine. Afterwards we will smoke cigarettes and talk over the Journalistic article. Could we go to your rooms, I am so far off, and clubs are difficult to talk in. This however is for you entirely to settle. Also send me your address again like a good fellow. I have lost it.

I think your number is excellent, but as usual had to go to St James's Street to get a copy. Even Grosvenor Place does not get the *C & S* till Thursday night! This is all wrong, isn't it. Truly yours                    OSCAR WILDE


## To Wemyss Reid[2]
MS. Hyde

[*18 May 1887*[3]]                    *16 Tite Street*

Dear Mr Wemyss Reid, I beg to accept the terms offered to me by Messrs Cassell for the editing of the *Lady's World*, and hope that with your help we will make it a success. Truly yours                    OSCAR WILDE

---

[1] Wilde's article "The Child Philosopher" appeared in the 20 April issue of the *Court and Society Review* and was reprinted in Mason.
[2] Journalist and biographer (1842–1905). General manager of Cassell's publishing firm 1887–1905. Founded the *Speaker* in 1890 and edited it until 1897. Knighted 1894.
[3] So dated in another hand.

## To Ellen Terry
MS. Smallhythe

[? July 1887][1]                                    16 Tite Street

Dear Ellen, Your love is more wonderful even than a crystal
caught in bent reeds of gold, and I don't envy Constance any
more, for I will wear the love, and no one shall see it. As for
the box — it will be the sweetest of pleasures to be the
guests of the Goddess — and oh! dear Ellen, look sometimes
in our direction, and let us come and pay due homage afterwards to the gracious lady and great artist we adore. Always
yours                                                    OSCAR


## To Alsagar Vian[2]

[Postmark 9 September 1887]                          16 Tite Street

Dear Vian, I will do *The Barrister*, the *Lyceum*, and
Buchanan's play for you. The latter is on Monday night.[3]
    Thank you for your letter. Very truly yours
                                          OSCAR WILDE


[1] It is impossible to date this letter, but we know that the Wildes attended
a performance of *The Merchant of Venice* at the Lyceum on 16 July
1887 (see *Letters*, p. 202).
[2] Text from a transcript in an unknown hand.
[3] Wilde's review of *The Winter's Tale* at the Lyceum, *The Barrister*,
a farcical comedy by George Manville Fenn and J.H. Darnley at the
Comedy Theatre, and *The Blue Bells of Scotland* by Robert Buchanan at
the Novelty Theatre, was published in the *Court and Society Review* of
14 September 1887, and reprinted in Mason.

68

# To Lady Gregory[1]

MS. Clark

[*September 1887*]                    *16 Tite Street*

Dear Lady Gregory, Will you allow me to add your name to the list of contributors to a monthly magazine I have been asked to edit for Cassell's the publishers?

I am anxious to make the magazine the recognised organ through which women of culture and position will express their views, and to which they will contribute.

The Princess Christian, Lady Portsmouth, Miss Thackeray, Mrs Francis Jeune, Lady Meath, Lady Wentworth, Mrs Fawcett, Mrs Craik, and others have promised to write, and a short article from your clever pen, on any subject you may select, would add a great charm to the magazine.

The magazine will appear under my editorship in November next, and will be illustrated by the best artists. I hope you will allow me to look forward to something of yours.

Pray remember me most kindly to Sir William, and believe me truly yours                    OSCAR WILDE

---

[1] Isabella Augusta Persse (1852–1932) married (1880) Sir William Gregory (1811–92), who had been Governor of Ceylon 1871–77. She later published books of Irish legends and many plays. With W.B. Yeats she was a founder of the Abbey Theatre in Dublin and of the Irish Players. She published no book before 1894 and did not contribute to the *Woman's World*.

## To Violet Fane[1]

*27 September 1887*                                      *16 Tite Street*

Dear Mrs Singleton, Your sonnet is really very beautiful, and I am very sorry that I was unable to come down and "crawl, a worm on Hazely Heath" — not that I was "strutting" at any "palace gate". I was in a troublesome editorial office, receiving frantic telegrams from Lady Archie Campbell about a correction I wished to make in her article.[2] It was a case of grammar versus mysticism, and the contest is still raging. I feel I shall have to yield.

I hope "the little poetesses" are well, and remain very sincerely yours                                      OSCAR WILDE

## To George Macmillan
MS. Macmillan

*[Mid-October 1887]*                                      *16 Tite Street*

Dear George, I am going to make literary criticism one of the features of the *Woman's World*, and to give special prominence to books written by women. Should you care to send me any books of the kind I will see that they are duly

---

[1] Mary Montgomerie Lamb (1843–1905), wife of H.L. Singleton. As Violet Fane she published poems, essays, novels and stories. Wilde's quotations are from her sonnet "Hazely Heath", which he published in the first (November 1887) number of the *Woman's World*. Text from catalogue of the City Book Auction of New York, March 1946.
[2] Janey Sevilla Callander (d.1923) married (1869) Lord Archibald Campbell, younger son of the eighth Duke of Argyll. She was a keen producer of pastoral plays, about which she wrote an article, "The Woodland Gods", which Wilde printed on the first pages of the first number of the *Woman's World*.

noticed — Lady Augusta Noel's[1] novel for instance, or Mrs Hartley's last book.[2]

How sad Mrs Craik's death is.[3] I was very shocked to hear of it, as I had heard from her only a few days before her death. Believe me truly yours      OSCAR WILDE

## To the Marchioness of Salisbury[4]
MS. Hatfield

[*Late October 1887*]          *16 Tite Street*

Mr Oscar Wilde presents his compliments to Lady Salisbury, and begs Lady Salisbury's acceptance of the first number of the *Woman's World*.[5]

Mr Wilde would esteem it a great honour if Lady Salisbury would write a short article on any social, political, or literary subject. Such an article from her pen would add charm and distinction to the magazine, and be of inestimable service in helping the magazine to attain the high position Mr Wilde is anxious to secure for it.[6]

[1] 1838–1902. Daughter of the sixth Earl of Albemarle. Her novel *Hithersea Mere* was published in three volumes by Macmillan in 1887 and reviewed by Wilde in the January 1888 issue of the *Woman's World*.
[2] *Ismay's Children* by Mrs May Hartley (née Laffan), published by Macmillan in 1887 and reviewed by Wilde in the December 1887 issue of the *Woman's World*.
[3] Mrs Craik (née Mulock 1826), author of *John Halifax, Gentleman* and many other novels, died suddenly on 12 October 1887. Wilde published a short appreciation of her in the November issue of the *Woman's World*. Her husband George Lillie Craik was a partner in Macmillan's.
[4] Georgina, née Alderson (1827–1899), wife of the third Marquess (1830–1903), the Conservative Prime Minister.
[5] Dated November 1887, but probably available in late October.
[6] Lady Salisbury contributed nothing to the *Woman's World*.

# To Wemyss Reid

MS. Clark

[? *Late 1887*]                                    *La Belle Sauvage*[1]

Dear Mr Reid, Madame Dieulafoy the well-known female explorer[2] has offered, in answer to a request of mine, to write four illustrated articles for the *Woman's World* for sixteen guineas an article. I would be content with *two*, or with one if necessary, but wish to know if the House would approve of so large a sum being paid to a writer.

She of course contributes drawings and unpublished photographs, so I think it would attract much notice from everyone.

I enclose her letter. Yours faithfully          OSCAR WILDE

# To Homer Watson[3]

*15 February 1888*                              [*16 Tite Street*]

My dear Mr Watson, The picture has finally arrived and I have much pleasure in telling you how pleased I am with it. It is quite what I desired from your hand, in tone and technique and feeling; the treatment of the sheep is excellent and the whole sense of rain and wind entirely free and delightful.

I have much pleasure in enclosing a cheque for $50. I hope to be able to get you some more commissions here, and I want to be able to have some day the pleasure of personally knowing one whose work gives me such great artistic pleasure. Believe me truly yours          OSCAR WILDE

[1] The address of Cassell's and the *Woman's World*.
[2] Jeanne Paule Henriette Rachel Dieulafoy, French archaeologist and writer (1851–1916). Nothing of hers appeared in the *Woman's World*.
[3] Canadian artist (1855–1936). Wilde, on his visit to Canada in 1882, had admired Watson's work and secured him several commissions. Text from *Oscar Wilde in Canada* by Kevin O'Brien (1982).

72

## To Mrs Richards[1]

MS. Clark

[*Postmark 19 March 1888*]                    *16 Tite Street*

Dear Mrs Richards, If I must, I must! The subject will be "Thomas Chatterton." I will come down by 11 o'clock train. Yours truly                                    OSCAR WILDE[2]


## To Florence Stoker[3]

[*June 1888*]

Dear Florrie, Will you give me the pleasure of accepting a copy of my book of fairy tales? I hope you will like them, simple though they are; and I think you will enjoy Crane's pretty pictures, and Jacomb Hood's designs. With kind regards to Bram                                    [OSCAR]


## To Blanche Medhurst

MS. Private

[*Summer 1888*]                               *16 Tite Street*

Dear Miss Medhurst, I think your article very interesting

---

[1] The wife of S. Wall Richards (see p. 65).

[2] On 7 April 1888 Wilde duly lectured on "Thomas Chatterton: the Boy-Poet of the Eighteenth Century" in the Shaftesbury Hall, Bournemouth.

[3] Née Florence Balcombe (1858–1937), Wilde's first love during his youthful days in Ireland. She married (1878) Bram Stoker (1847–1912), Irving's manager at the Lyceum Theatre and the author of *Dracula* (1897). This letter accompanied a copy of *The Happy Prince and Other Tales* (published in May 1888). It is inscribed "Florence Stoker from her friend the author Oscar Wilde June '88". Book and letter together fetched $8500 at Christie's, New York, on 16 November 1984. Text from Christie's catalogue.

and it deals with a problem that confronts us every day. I will hope to use it in an early number.[1]

I think, if you will allow me to say so, that it is hardly accurate to say that the care of children was due to Christianity: the Greeks and Romans were distinguished for their love of children: it is part of their civilization: in fact the *misery* of children is a modern thing entirely, and due to economic causes such as over-population, and over-production. It is a small point, not worth correcting.

I think there could be no objection to your writing on the Mormons again — you know them so well that it will be easy to give different subject-matter: 3000 (three thousand) words will be quite sufficient, as I should like the article illustrated. Have you any photographs? If so I should be very much obliged if you would lend them to me.[2] Believe me truly yours                                    OSCAR WILDE

## To Oscar Browning[3]
MS. Hyde

[*October 1888*]                                    *16 Tite Street*

My dear O.B., Thanks for your letter. A short article on Goethe's house with photographs would be delightful — *3000* words quite sufficient. If you send me the photographs

---

[1] Her article "Playgrounds and Open Spaces", which appeared in the September 1888 issue of the *Woman's World*.
[2] Blanche Medhurst's illustrated article "The Disintegration of Mormonism" appeared in the April 1890 issue of the *Woman's World*, after Wilde's editorship was over.
[3] 1837–1923. Eton master 1860–75, Cambridge don and "character" 1876–1909. His only contribution to the *Woman's World* was a feeble sonnet on Bournemouth.

I will get them reproduced at once, so as to have no delay about the publication.

I knew you would like Bobbie Ross.[1] He is charming, and as clever as can be, with excellent taste and sound knowledge. I am so glad he is with you. I know no one who has a more intellectual influence than yourself: to be ranked amongst your friends is, for anyone, a liberal education. Ever yours                                                            OSCAR

## To J. Graham Hill[2]
MS. Mason

[? 1888]                                                            16 Tite Street

My dear Graham Hill, I am charmed with your little volume;[3] the triolets, ballades, and rondeaus are very graceful and dainty. I am sorry you have rhymed "tears" to "ideas" in your envoy; rhymes of this kind are very wicked, but you certainly have a light touch and a pleasant fancy.

The book is very prettily got up, and "M.L.",[4] whoever she is, should feel quite proud at such an artistic offering. Are you very much in love with M.L.? and does M.L. love you?

Come and see me some day. Wednesday afternoon usually finds me in. Truly yours                                       OSCAR WILDE

[1] Robert Baldwin Ross, literary journalist and art-critic (1869–1918). Canadian-born. Went up to King's College, Cambridge in 1888. Wilde's most faithful friend. Usually called Robbie.
[2] Poet, journalist and playwright (1865–1933). His play *Havana*, with music by Leslie Stuart, was a great success at the Gaiety in 1908.
[3] *Under Her Window* (1888).
[4] Matilda (Minnie) Lloyd, whom Hill later married.

## To J. Graham Hill
### MS. Mason

[*? 1888*]                                                *16 Tite Street*

Dear Graham Hill, I don't think that poems are ever really
helped by the publication of letters from private friends. An
anonymous criticism is always something, or supposed to
be something, but personal letters are different. However
you are quite at liberty to do as you think best.

I hope you will be successful in whatever branch of
literature you take up, and am very glad you are turning
your attention to prose. Good prose is what we want. How
is your journalism progressing? Truly yours

OSCAR WILDE


## To Arthur Clifton[1]
### MS. Clark

[*Postmark 4 December 1888*]                       *16 Tite Street*

My dear Arthur, Thank you for your letter and your telegram. I was very much disappointed of course, but we must
have an evening together soon.

I can lend you a book by Brander Mathews with an essay
on Austin Dobson.[2]

I wish you would send me two or three of your poems.
You have certainly a delicate ear for music, and perhaps

---

[1] 1862–1932. At this time a solicitor. Later an art-dealer.
[2] *Pen and Ink* (1888) by the American critic (1852–1929). Henry Austin
Dobson (1840–1921) had by now completed his best work as a poet and
was rapidly establishing himself as biographer and belles-lettrist. His
biography of Oliver Goldsmith was published in 1888.

some day you will give us something as perfect as the first three verses of the Greek Girl.[1] Ever yours OSCAR WILDE

Shall we dine on *Tuesday*?

## To Douglas Sladen[2]
MS. Mason

[*c. December 1888*]                                                    *16 Tite Street*

Dear Mr Sladen, I am afraid that I hardly know any young American poets — they come and go, but abide not. You will however have no difficulty in Boston in meeting whoever is worth meeting.

The best of the young poets is Edgar Fawcett.[3] I think him the best American poet there is — alive — but he is furious with me because I never answer his letters. If you are publishing an anthology you should not fail to use his work largely.

Call on John Boyle O'Reilly at Boston — he is a delightful fellow. Truly yours                                           OSCAR WILDE

The poet Roberts of Canada is admirable.[4]

[1] "To a Greek Girl", a poem by Dobson, first published in the *Spectator* on 8 May 1875 and included in Dobson's *Proverbs in Porcelain* (1877).
[2] Prolific hack who wrote dozens of books on many subjects (1856–1947). His *Younger American Poets* appeared in 1891. On 14 December 1888 Wilde reviewed his *Australian Poets, 1788–1888* in the *Pall Mall Gazette*. He described it as "an extraordinary collection of mediocrities whom Mr Sladen has somewhat ruthlessly dragged from their modest and well-merited obscurity".
[3] 1847–1904. The *Concise Dictionary of American Biography* says that he "satirised New York society in some thirty-five tepid novels and plays", but Sladen described him as a master of irony, with an extraordinary command of metre and rhyme.
[4] Charles George Douglas Roberts (1860–1943) published almost as many books as Douglas Sladen. Knighted 1935. Wilde was probably recommending him as editor of a selection of *Younger Canadian Poets* as an appendix to the *American Poets*.

## To W.T. Stead[1]

MS. Private

[*Late December 1888*]

Dear Mr Stead, Joseph Skipsey, the Tyneside poet (once a miner and now the caretaker of a school), has asked me to forward the accompanying volume of his poems to you. I reviewed him for the *P.M.G.* last year and he seems to have been much pleased with the notice. There is much in his work that is good and fine, and some of the little lyrics are delightful in their freshness and freedom.[2]

I am still mourning over the Brobdingnagian size of the *Pall Mall*. But I suppose it is no use repining.[3] Truly yours

OSCAR WILDE

## To Alice Corkran[4]

MS. Hyde

[*c. 1888*]                                             *16 Tite Street*

My dear Alice, I think your friend's little book quite delightful, and I will be very pleased if she will write me an article of 3000 words on Economical French Cookery, giving practical hints to English housewives. As regards your own article, everything that you write is full of grace and delicacy of literary style, so I hope you will do your account of the

---

[1] William Thomas Stead (1849–1912), journalist and author. In 1883 he succeeded John Morley as editor of the *Pall Mall Gazette*. Drowned in the *Titanic*.

[2] See above, p. 65.

[3] The format of the *Pall Mall Gazette* was enlarged on 1 January 1889, but advance copies or dummies of that issue may have been available in late December 1888.

[4] Author and journalist (d.1916).

*Retreat.* (I suppose it was in a Protestant or an English Catholic convent? A *Roman* Catholic convent will hardly do.) There is a good deal to be said about the necessity of a retreat especially for literary people, but I think that it should not be religious — merely a retirement from the world for a short season. To Wordsworth the Lakes were a retreat, and the idea of standing aloof from practical life is constantly appearing in Greek philosophy.

Pray remember me to your mother and Henriette,[1] and believe me truly yours                                   OSCAR WILDE


## To Elizabeth Robins[2]
MS. Clark

[*Early January 1889*]                                   *16 Tite Street*

Dear Miss Robins, My best and sincerest congratulations to you on your great success: you have definitely asserted your position as an actress of the first order, and revealed yourself as an artist of a very rare and sensitive temperament, and of quick imaginative insight into the dramatic modes by which life can find expression. The play was second-rate and provincial; but there was nothing but praise and enthusiasm for you. Your future on our stage is assured. Believe me, with renewed congratulations, your sincere admirer

OSCAR WILDE


[1] Alice's sister.
[2] American actress and writer (1862–1952). Her first major appearance on the English stage was in January 1889, when she took over matinée performances in the part of Mrs Errol ("Dearest") in a brief revival of Frances Hodgson Burnett's *The Real Little Lord Fauntleroy*, her adaptation of her famous novel.

# To Henry Lucy[1]

[*c. 5 January 1889*]                                    *16 Tite Street*

Thanks for the charming reference to my *Fortnightly* article:[2] but I fear Fauntleroy[3] is not so fascinating as Wainewright, and my *Nineteenth Century* article[4] is so much the better of the two that I should like to know your views on my new theory of art contained in it.

# To George Macmillan
MS. Macmillan

[*January 1889*]                                        *16 Tite Street*

My dear George, Thank you for your letter and its enclosure, for which I send receipt.

The article was written in March 1886 at Carr's[5] request, and I could not get a proof of it till last June. Finally in November last I wrote to Carr to say that I was going to publish it in my own magazine, and I am afraid that its appearance in the *English Illustrated* is entirely due to that terrible

---

[1] Parliamentary correspondent of *Punch* and the *Daily News* (1843–1924). Knighted 1909. Text from a bookseller's catalogue.
[2] "Pen, Pencil, and Poison: A Study" on the life of the poisoner Thomas Griffiths Wainewright (1794–1852). Published in the January 1889 issue of the *Fortnightly Review. Punch* noticed it on 5 January.
[3] Henry Fauntleroy (1785–1824), a banker who was hanged for forgery. Lucy, in his book *Nearing Jordan* (1916), writes: "At one time the story of Fauntleroy . . . had a predominant fascination for Wilde. He contemplated writing his biography."
[4] "The Decay of Lying: a Dialogue" in the January 1889 issue of the *Nineteenth Century*. Both essays were collected in Wilde's *Intentions* (1891).
[5] Joseph Comyns Carr, dramatist, critic and editor (1849–1916).

threat.[1] For an article written on commission it was certainly kept too long. I am however very pleased that it has been so popular as I hear it is. My little story of "The Happy Prince," which perhaps you have read, languished in the manuscript chest of the same magazine for eighteen months — but I finally got it back. I fear I must take to writing on Coaching Days! This is the only subject that ensures publication. Sincerely yours                                                    OSCAR WILDE

## To *Walter Hamilton*[2]
### TS. Clark

[*Postmark 29 January 1889*]                                    *16 Tite Street*

Dear Mr Hamilton, I have never collected the parodies of my work in poetry. Collecting contemporaneous things is like trying to hold froth in a sieve. The *New York World* of January 1882 had some admirable parodies, as well as I remember, but as most of my poems are long and lyrical, they have not, I fancy, been good models. I think the numbers of your book which you have kindly sent are most interesting, and parody, which is the Muse with her tongue in her cheek, has always amused me; but it requires a light touch, a fanciful treatment, and, oddly enough, a love of the poet whom it caricatures. One's disciples can parody one — nobody else. Yours sincerely                                    OSCAR WILDE

[1] "London Models" appeared in the January 1889 issue of the *English Illustrated Magazine*, which was edited by Joseph Comyns Carr and published by Macmillan. It was illustrated by Harper Pennington. The article was reprinted in *Miscellanies*.

[2] English writer and book-collector (1844–99). His book *The Aesthetic Movement in England* (1882) discussed Wilde's early life and theories, and his *Parodies of English and American Authors* (6 vols, 1884–89), for which he was still collecting material, included several parodies of Wilde's work. The six volumes were first issued in separate parts or "numbers". An incomplete text of this letter appeared in *Letters*.

## To May Morris[1]

MS. Clark

[Mid-April 1889]                                    16 Tite Street

Dear Miss Morris, I am afraid I could not promise to attend any committee meetings, as I am very busy, but if you think my name of any service pray make any use of it you like.

I put a short notice of the lectures into the *Daily Telegraph* and the *Pall Mall*, mentioned you as organising secretary. I thought a note in the *Telegraph* would be of service, as a means of explaining to people that the subject of the lectures was *not* to be "Anarchy with practical illustrations". My own magazine (May number) went to press three weeks ago — otherwise you would have had any notice you like. I suppose June would be too late? Truly yours

OSCAR WILDE

## To Justin Huntly McCarthy[2]

MS. Clark

[Mid-May 1889]

Dear Justin, Your book is charming, and your prose worthy of the sinless master whom mortals call Flaubert. I see a new Omar in a new tent, and while I love FitzGerald as you do,

---

[1] 1862–1938. Younger daughter of William Morris, poet, artist, manufacturer and Socialist (1834–96). She was as active a Socialist as her father. The note in the *Daily Telegraph* of 12 April 1889 announced that she was arranging a series of lectures by Prince Peter Kropotkin on Social Evolution. The Prince (1842–1921) was a Russian author, geographer and anarchist. Wilde wrote appreciatively of him in his *De Profundis* letter (see *Letters*, p. 488).

[2] Dramatist, novelist, historian and Irish Nationalist M.P. (1861–1936).

I am fascinated by your strange purple and fresh amethyst.[1]

Certainly for wisdom we must go to the East, and it is pleasant to go with you as one's torch-bearer.

Only one thing I regret — the mention of Quilter in the preface — it seems wrong: Omar would not have liked it.[2] But they say there is grit in every pearl-oyster. Certainly your book has many pearls, so *je me console*. Ever yours

OSCAR WILDE


## Telegram: To Clyde Fitch[3]
MS. Hyde

[*Postmark 22 June 1889*]                                    *Chelsea*

What a charming day it has been.                         OSCAR


## To Mrs R.B. Cunninghame Graham[4]
MS. Edinburgh

[*c. 30 June 1889*]                                    *16 Tite Street*

Dear Mrs Cunninghame Graham, I wish so much I could

---

[1] McCarthy's prose translation of *The Rubaiyat of Omar Khayyam* was published in May 1889.

[2] In his preface McCarthy gave details of an unauthorised and privately printed edition of FitzGerald's translation organised in 1887 by Harry Quilter, art-critic and Whistler's *bête noire* (1851–1907).

[3] Prolific and successful American dramatist (1865–1909).

[4] Gabriela de la Balmondière (1860–1906) eloped at the age of eighteen with Robert Bontine Cunninghame Graham, who was twenty-six (see note p. 165). It was a very happy marriage. She published poems, stories and translations. On Tuesday, 2 July 1889, she lectured to the Bloomsbury Socialist Club on "The Ideals of Socialism". She spoke as a Socialist and a Roman Catholic, attacking Liberalism and Protestantism, and insisting on the complete political emancipation of women. She was strongly opposed by Karl Marx's daughter, Eleanor Marx Aveling.

come and hear you on Tuesday, but I am dining out. I think your subject most interesting, but what is to become of an indolent hedonist like myself if Socialism and the Church join forces against me? I want to stand apart, and look on, being neither for God nor for his enemies. This, I hope, will be allowed.

Seriously speaking, however, what I want to see is a reconciliation of Socialism with Science. Ritchie, in his *Darwinism and Politics*, has tried to do this, but his book, which I suppose you have seen, is very slight and amateurish.[1]

Give my love to your delightful and dangerous husband.
Ever yours                                                    OSCAR WILDE


## To Henry Lucy
MS. Mason

[*c. 6 July 1889*]                                           *Lyric Club*

Dear Lucy, Many thanks for a most fascinating invitation. Unluckily I will be out of town then, so cannot come.

By diligently reading between the lines of *Punch* I have come to the conclusion that you are really converted to "Mr Will Hewes". Pray don't undeceive me, as I should like to consider you a convert.[2] Ever yours          OSCAR WILDE

---

[1] David George Ritchie, philosopher (1853–1903), published *Darwinism and Politics* in 1889, and Wilde had reviewed it in the May 1889 issue of the *Woman's World*.

[2] In *The Portrait of Mr W.H.* (first published in *Blackwood's Magazine*, June 1889) Wilde had sought to prove that the mysterious dedicatee of the first published edition of Shakespeare's Sonnets was a young actor called William Hughes or Hewes. On 6 July 1889 Lucy, in his regular *Punch* page "Essence of Parliament", invented a brief dialogue between "Toby" (i.e. himself) and Lord Pembroke, in which they mentioned Wilde's theory.

## To Lawrence Barrett[1]
### MS. Texas

*[Early July 1889]*                                        *16 Tite Street*

My dear Mr Barrett, I am very proud and pleased to learn that you have not forgotten *The Duchess of Padua*. I should be very glad to make any alterations in it you can suggest, and indeed I have no doubt that the play could be vastly improved.

I could go to Kreuznach[2] at the end of this month for five or six days, but would it be impossible to arrange the alterations by correspondence? I do not know what the expense of the journey is, and have not much money to spare. Your kind offer to be your guest I accept with great pleasure.

It is right to tell you that before I received your letter Miss Calhoun[3] had approached me on the subject of the play. But nothing is settled, as she has, as yet, made me no offer.

Personally I would sooner that my work should be presented to the public by an artist of your experience and knowledge. I know how very perfect all your productions are, and what unity of effect you have been able to present by means of right balance and artistic tact. *Francesca da Rimini*, which I saw in New York, always remains in my memory as one of the best modern productions of our stage.[4]

[1] American actor-manager (1838–91). In 1882 he had made Wilde "a very large offer" (*Letters*, p. 127) for *The Duchess of Padua*, but Wilde turned it down, because he had written the play for Mary Anderson and wanted her to play the name-part. In 1883 she decided against it. For Barrett's production of the play in January 1891, see pp. 92 and 104.
[2] A watering-place on the river Nahe in the Rhineland, where presumably Barrett was taking the cure. Wilde duly paid a brief visit to Kreuznach (see *Letters*, p. 248).
[3] Eleanor Calhoun, American actress (1865–1927).
[4] On 27 August 1882 Barrett produced at the Star Theatre, New York, an adaptation of the blank-verse drama *Francesca da Rimini* (1855) by the American poet and dramatist George Henry Boker (1823–90), and it remained in Barrett's repertory for years.

As well as I can see, I could start about the 19th of July, and be back here before the end of the month. I suppose Kreuznach is not very far? My German geography is disgraceful.

Should Miss Calhoun make me a definite offer, I will let you know before I accept it.

I hope your family are all well, and remain your most sincere friend                                        OSCAR WILDE


## To Wemyss Reid
MS. Hyde

[*September–October 1889*]                              *16 Tite Street*

Dear Mr Reid, Now that my term of editorship is ended, I am anxious to express through you my thanks to the firm for the courtesy with which they have always treated me.[1]

I am specially indebted to Mr Bale, whose artistic knowledge and experience have always been at my disposal,[2] and to Mr Williams[3] who has always helped me with advice and suggestion. Indeed from the Heads of each Department I have received every possible attention and mark of kindness, and I think it right to say that I found Mr Fish a most reliable and intelligent sub-editor.[4]

I hope that my connection with the firm is not entirely ended, and thanking you personally for the help and encouragement you have always given me, I remain very sincerely yours                                                OSCAR WILDE

[1] The October 1889 issue of the *Woman's World* was the last edited by Wilde.
[2] Edwin Bale (1838–1923), water-colour artist. Art Director of Cassell & Co Ltd 1882–86.
[3] John Williams, chief editor at Cassell's.
[4] Arthur Fish, journalist (1860–1940), was Wilde's assistant editor on the *Woman's World*.

## To J.M. Stoddart[1]
### MS. Clark[2]

[*Date of receipt 17 December 1889*]          *16 Tite Street*

Dear Mr Stoddart, Thanks for your letter. I am glad to say that I am much better now: it was an attack of malaria, that enervating and wretched malady.

I have invented a new story, which is better than "The Fisherman and his Soul,"[3] and I am quite ready to set to work at once on it. It will be ready by the end of March. But I would ask you to let me have half the honorarium in advance — £100 — as I have a great many offers of work, and having been idle for four months require some money. I hope you will let me have this as soon as possible.

Believe me with kind regards ever yours

OSCAR WILDE

## To an Unidentified Publisher
### MS. Buffalo

[*May 1890*]          *16 Tite Street*

Dear Sir, I have waited till I could make you some practical offer of work. On the 20th of next month there appears in *Lippincott's Magazine* a one-volume novel of mine, 50,000 words in length.[4] After three months the copyright reverts to

---

[1] On 30 August 1889 Stoddart, who was now managing editor of *Lippincott's Magazine*, had entertained Wilde and Conan Doyle to dinner in London. He asked them both for stories he could publish. Doyle replied with *The Sign of Four*, his second Sherlock Holmes novel, which appeared in *Lippincott's* in February 1890. Wilde's "new story" was *The Picture of Dorian Gray*, which appeared there in July 1890.
[2] Replacing fragment in *Letters*, p. 251.
[3] First published in *A House of Pomegranates* (1891).
[4] *The Picture of Dorian Gray.*

me, and I propose to publish it, with two new chapters, as a novel. I want you to read it, and to see if you would like to undertake the publication. I think it will make a sensation.

I also have a volume of essays and dialogues which I wish to bring out in the autumn.[1] But the novel is of course quite new, and I should like to have it brought out by you. I must thank you for the courtesy you have shown me in the other matter, and hope to begin a connection with your firm. I remain truly yours                                     OSCAR WILDE

## To the Editor of the Scots Observer
MS. Private

[*Postmark 25 July 1890*]                              *16 Tite Street*

Dear Sir, My letter[2] was posted on Wednesday, and it must have been delayed by some gross carelessness on the part of the Post Office. I return it to you now corrected.

Unless it is a formal rule of the paper to represent correspondents as signing themselves "Yours etc.," I wish you would sign my letters as they are written. No gentleman ever signs "Yours etc." Yours faithfully   OSCAR WILDE[3]

[1] *Intentions.*
[2] See *Letters*, p. 268.
[3] Wilde's first letter to the *Scots Observer*, attacking their review of *Dorian Gray* (*Letters*, pp. 265–7), appeared there ending "I am, etc."

## To *Arthur Howard Pickering*[1]
MS. Clark

[*Late July 1890*]                                     *16 Tite Street*

My dear Pickering, We are all angry with you for not coming over. When the lilacs blossom and the laburnum hangs its dusty gold over the railings of our London squares we look for our American friends, and so we look for you. Come in the autumn, and we will ask the laburnum to grow honey-coloured for your pleasure.

I am charmed you like *Dorian Gray*. It is my best piece of work, and I hope to make it still better, when it appears in book form.

The fatal book that Lord Henry lent Dorian is one of my many unwritten works. Some day I must go through the formality of putting it on paper.

My wife and my mother both send you their kindest and most affectionate greetings. So does your sincere friend

OSCAR WILDE

## To *F. Holland Day*[2]
MS. Hyde

[*Postmark 11 August 1890*]                           *16 Tite Street*

Dear Sir, I send you a copy of my sonnet on the sale of Keats's love-letters: it was published in William Sharp's first edition of *Sonnets of this Century*[3] (Walter Scott pub-

---

[1] Pickering, a friend of the American dramatist Clyde Fitch, had written from Roxbury, Massachusetts, on 7 July, praising *The Picture of Dorian Gray* on its appearance in *Lippincott's Magazine*.

[2] Wealthy and eccentric American publisher, photographer, and collector of everything to do with Keats (1864–1933). Founded the publishing firm of Copeland & Day in 1893. Bequeathed Fanny Brawne's letters to Fanny Keats to Keats House in Hampstead.

[3] Published in 1886.

89

lisher) but was subsequently removed by a timorous editor, on account of a review in the *Spectator* which described it as 'blasphemy': which is, I believe, the only instance of the *Spectator* influencing any body on any thing.[1]

I should be most pleased to have a photograph of the bust of Keats you mention. Keats's grandniece, Miss Speed, whom I met in Kentucky (what a pen!), was an ugly likeness of the poet — had something of his fine fierceness, though little of his rapt ardour. Her lips were like his.[2]

I will be at home the next three mornings (11–1). Come, if you are idle, and bring the photograph. Faithfully yours

OSCAR WILDE

These are the letters that Endymion wrote
To one he loved in secret and apart:
And now the brawlers of the auction-mart
Bargain and bid for each poor blotted note,
Ay! for each separate pulse of passion quote
The merchant's price:- I think, they love not Art
Who break the crystal of a poet's heart
That small and sickly eyes may glare or gloat.
Is it not said that many years ago
In a far Eastern town some soldiers ran
With torches through the midnight, and began
To wrangle for mean raiment, and to throw
Dice for the garments of a wretched man,
Not knowing the God's wonder, or his woe?

OSCAR WILDE

"*Midnight*" is wrong: is it not? Christ was taken down at sunset I believe. But I don't think I can change it: I like "ran with torches through the midnight": besides I don't

---

[1] The *Spectator* review of 6 March 1886 picked out Wilde's sonnet as "very hysterical" and referred to its author's "disgusting audacity" and "downright irreverence".
[2] See *Letters*, p. 108.

90

suppose they gambled when on guard. How sordid these realistic considerations are! It comes from having recklessly written a novel. I am ashamed of them.

P.S. Sonnet first appeared in *Dramatic Review*.[1]


## To Arthur Galton[2]
MS. Montague

[*October 1890*]                                    *16 Tite Street*

Dear Galton, Your Tacitus is a charming little book, and your preface, like everything you write, very perfect in its sanity of wise criticism and good English. Many thanks for your gift. I still hope that Tiberius was very wicked, but fear that philology was his only crime. Ever yours

OSCAR WILDE


## To Lawrence Barrett
MS. Montague

[*Late 1890*]                                    *16 Tite Street*

Dear Lawrence Barrett, I accept your offer with very great pleasure, and I count myself fortunate in placing my play in the hands of so distinguished an artist as yourself.

If not inconvenient to you, it would render me a service if you would let me have £100 now, to serve as the instalment due on the day of its production, or as the forfeit in

[1] On 23 January 1886.
[2] Arthur Howard Galton (1852–1921), editor of *The Reign of Tiberius, Out of the First Six Annals of Tacitus*, translated by T. Gordon and published by Walter Scott in the Camelot Classics in October 1890.

case of the play not being brought out. It is rather important for me to have some money just at present.

With regard to the cutting of the play I should be very happy to condense it on lines suggested by you, or to leave that in your hands.

I hope you are now quite recovered: I often think of a delightful drive we had on the hills over the Rhine.

Thanking you for the appreciation you have always shown of my work, and for many kindnesses, I remain very sincerely yours OSCAR WILDE

With regard to the title of the play — it would be well to alter it, so as to preserve the secret of authorship perfectly.[1]

[1] When Barrett produced *The Duchess of Padua*, it was retitled *Guido Ferranti* and carried no author's name. It opened at the Broadway Theatre, New York, on 26 January 1891, and ran only until 14 February.

# LONDON III

1891-95

## To H.S.H. The Princess of Monaco[1]
MS. Hyde

[*Late February 1891*]                    *Hôtel de l'Athénée* [*Paris*]

Dear Princess, Many thanks for your charming and gracious
letter, which I have just received. I am miserable at missing
the delightful evening you offer me, but I am sorry to say I
am still almost without voice, and without voice one cannot
even listen with appreciation, or look with the pleasure of
expressing one's admiration. I had intended to write to you
this morning, but not hearing from you thought you might
have left for the south. Will you allow me to call tomorrow
in the afternoon to pay my respects and offer my homage,
even though it be in dumb-show? I should be so sorry not to
see you while I am in Paris.

  Believe me, dear Princess, sincerely yours

                                    OSCAR WILDE


## To Mrs W.H. Grenfell[2]
MS. Grenfell

[*Late April 1891*]                                *16 Tite Street*

Dear Mrs Grenfell, I am afraid that by June 3rd poor Hedda
will have given up looking for scarlet sensations in a drab-

---

[1] Alice (1858–1925), wife of the Prince of Monaco, was a great patron
of art and artists. Wilde dedicated his story "The Fisherman and his
Soul" (in *A House of Pomegranates*) to her.
[2] Ethel (Ettie) Fane (1868–1952), granddaughter of the eleventh Earl of
Westmorland, married (1887) William Henry Grenfell (1855–1945),
all-round athlete and Liberal Member of Parliament. He was created
Lord Desborough in 1905. Their home was at Taplow Court on the
Thames near Maidenhead. Their eldest son was Julian Grenfell, the
author of "Into Battle" and other poems.

coloured existence.[1] I went there on Thursday night, and the house was dreary — the pit full of sad vegetarians, and the stalls occupied by men in mackintoshes and women in knitted shawls of red wool. So at least it seemed to me. However, we might go to *L'Enfant Prodigue*[2] or *The Dancing Girl*[3] — but is it necessary to go anywhere? Why not a little dinner? You, Lady Elcho[4], Arthur Balfour[5] and myself. It would be entrancing and delightful. But of course I would go anywhere with pleasure, and June 3rd is set apart for a delightful evening.

How nice of you to ask us to Taplow. I look forward to a charming Sunday. Believe me very truly yours

OSCAR WILDE

## To W.L. Courtney[6]
MS. Hyde

[*c. 19 May 1891*]                                                 *16 Tite Street*

My dear Courtney, I think I detected your pleasant friendly touch in the review of my essays that appeared in the *Daily Telegraph*.[7] In any case I write to ask you whether my novel

[1] Ibsen's *Hedda Gabler* was produced at the Vaudeville Theatre from 20 to 24 April 1891, with Elizabeth Robins in the title-role.
[2] A play in mime by Michel Carré *fils*, music by André Wormser, which opened at the Prince of Wales's Theatre on 31 March 1891.
[3] A play in four acts by Henry Arthur Jones, which opened at the Haymarket Theatre on 15 January 1891, with Beerbohm Tree and Julia Neilson in the leading parts.
[4] Mary Constance Wyndham (1862–1937), married Lord Elcho, later Lord Wemyss (1857–1937).
[5] Conservative politician and writer on philosophy (1848–1930). At this time Chief Secretary for Ireland. Prime Minister 1902–5.
[6] Author and journalist (1850–1928). He joined the *Daily Telegraph* in 1890, and soon became Literary Editor and chief dramatic critic, a position he held until 1925. *The Picture of Dorian Gray* was published in book form in April 1891 and Wilde's book of essays *Intentions* on 2 May.
[7] On 19 May 1891.

of *Dorian Gray* could not be noticed also in the paper. The reason I ask it is this: when it first appeared it was very grossly and foolishly assailed as an immoral book, and I am anxious to have it treated purely from the art-standpoint: from the standpoint of style, plot, construction, psychology, and the like. From this standpoint much, no doubt, may be urged against it. Every true critic has his own temperament by whose laws he abides, and I may candidly admit that I admire my own work far too much to ask other people to praise it. But one does want, especially in England, to have one's work treated from the proper point of view. Could you do this for me? Of course I know your reviews are quite brief. That doesn't matter.[1] Very sincerely yours

OSCAR WILDE


## To Richard Le Gallienne[2]
MS. Hyde

[*June 1891*]                                           *16 Tite Street*

My dearest poet and always-loved friend, I forget Hamilton:[3] but send me your notice and I will correct facts if necessary. Of course note the new departure of "The Decay of Lying".[4] I am so glad you are going to do me. In haste, ever yours

OSCAR


[1] Courtney duly obliged with a brief notice on 15 June 1891.
[2] Poet, journalist and littérateur (1866–1947).
[3] i.e. What Walter Hamilton had written about him in *The Aesthetic Movement in England* (1882).
[4] In *Intentions*, where the essay had been rewritten since its appearance in the *Nineteenth Century* in 1889. Le Gallienne's review of *Intentions* appeared in the *Academy* on 4 July 1891 and was reprinted in *Oscar Wilde: The Critical Heritage* (1970).

## To Mrs W.H. Grenfell

MS. Grenfell

*[Late June 1891]* *16 Tite Street*

Dear Mrs Grenfell, You were so kind as to offer me a place in your collection of photographs at Taplow,[1] so I send you one which has the ordinary realistic quality of resemblance, a quality that in art gives me no pleasure. I feel that had I been consulted on the subject I would have produced a very different design for the author of *Intentions*. However, here it is: all that I would like to say about it is that my button-hole was much more charming than it appears: it was really very carefully thought out.

Lady Cowper's silence fills me with apprehension.[2] Am I in real disgrace? I hope not. I don't like lecturing. All lectures are tainted with a didactic element. Will you try and make my peace? I am quite wretched about it. Yours very sincerely                                    OSCAR WILDE

## To Mrs W.H. Grenfell

MS. Grenfell

*[Early July 1891]* *16 Tite Street*

Dear Mrs Grenfell, I am sending you a little book that contains a story, two stories in fact, that I told you at Taplow.[3] The book is No 1 of the Taplow Library: the others will be better.

---

[1] The only day on which Wilde signed the Taplow visitors' book was Sunday 31 May 1891.
[2] Katrine (1845–1913), daughter of the fourth Marquess of Northampton, married (1870) the seventh and last Earl Cowper (1834–1905). His sister was Mrs Grenfell's mother.
[3] *Lord Arthur Savile's Crime and other Stories* (July 1891).

98

I am feeling a little better than I did last week, Lady Cowper having written me a charming letter, which, entirely by reading between the lines, I have construed into a complete forgiveness — a plenary absolution for my dreadful behaviour about the lecture. At any rate I am to go to Wrest[1] after all, and that is a delightful prospect, which consoles me for some, I thought, rather severe remarks made on the subject yesterday afternoon by Lady Betty[2] on the terrace of the House of Commons. However, to be lectured for not lecturing is, I suppose, only fair.

I hope the stories will amuse you. Read them in the country some lovely evening under a tree, not in town. They have too much of town in them. Believe me sincerely yours

OSCAR WILDE

## *To Joseph Anderson*[3]

MS. Lockwood

[? *Mid-September 1891*]                    *16 Tite Street*

My dear Joe, I think after you have read the play[4] you had better let me have it back, as I would like to touch it up a little before Daly[5] sees it. Could you, if you have had time

---

[1] Wrest Park, near Ampthill in Bedfordshire, the country home of Lord and Lady Cowper. Wilde's visit there was on 1 August 1891.

[2] Almost certainly Lady Betty Balfour (1867–1942), daughter of the first Earl of Lytton (Wilde's friend to whom he dedicated *Lady Windermere's Fan*) and wife of Gerald Balfour, later second Earl Balfour (1853–1945).

[3] 1863–?1943. Actor. Brother of the American actress Mary Anderson. He married Gertrude, daughter of Lawrence Barrett, and their son Lawrence Anderson (1893–1939) became a leading London actor.

[4] *Lady Windermere's Fan*, then called *A Good Woman*.

[5] Augustin Daly, American theatre-director and impresario (1839–99). He declined *A Good Woman* (see *Letters*, p. 296). There is no proof that this letter is to Anderson, but the references to someone of his name on p. 104 suggest that he was dealing with American theatre-managers on Wilde's behalf.

to read it, bring it to Tite Street tomorrow at 12 o'clock and give me your advice about it. Afterwards we could lunch here. Send me a line, or a wire. Sincerely yours

OSCAR WILDE

## To Mrs W.H. Grenfell

MS. Grenfell

[*Postmark of receipt 12 November 1891*]
*29 Boulevard des Capucines, Paris*

Dear Mrs Grenfell, I hear from Lady de Grey[1] that you are going to India this winter! This seems to me very dreadful, as I suppose I shall not have the chance of seeing you for ages.

I am publishing shortly a new volume of fairy tales, rather like my *Happy Prince*, which perhaps you know, only more elaborate. One of the stories, which is about the little pale Infanta whom Velasquez painted, I have dedicated to you, as a slight return for that entrancing day at Taplow.[2] When do you leave for India? I fear the book will not be out for a fortnight or three weeks, and I want you to see it and to like it.

Paris is so charming that I think of becoming a French poet! Sincerely yours
OSCAR WILDE

[1] 1859–1917. Formerly Lady Lonsdale. See *Letters*, p. 65.
[2] "The Birthday of the Infanta" in *A House of Pomegranates*, published in November 1891.

## To Ernest Raynaud[1]
### MS. Hyde

[*Postmark 29 November 1891*] *29 Boulevard des Capucines*

Cher Monsieur Raynaud, Permettez moi de vous offrir tous mes remerciements les plus sincères de m'avoir fait l'honneur de me donner votre exquis et charmant volume dont la rare et troublante beauté me fascine et m'ensorcelle.

Certes, sur des "sujets modernes" vous avez fait des "vers antiques", et si les anciens voudraient apprendre quelque chose sur notre vie contemporaine c'est à vous qu'il faudrait aller. Ils aimeraient beaucoup le miel et la musique de votre flûte. Les Grecs trouveraient un Grec, les poètes un poète.

Je vous remercie encore une fois, et je vous prie d'agréer l'assurance de mes sentiments les plus distingués. J'espère qu'avant que je quitte Paris nous nous reverrons.

OSCAR WILDE


## To Albert Sterner[2]
### MS. Morgan

[*November or December 1891*] *29 Boulevard des Capucines*

My dear Sterner, This is a little line to wish you *bon voyage*, and to tell you how much I enjoyed our evenings together, and what a real pleasure it was for me to meet and know you. When you come back I will come over to Paris and sit for you with pleasure for a real Holbein portrait. It is sure to be a fine and distinguished thing.

In the meantime I hope you will accept a copy of *Dorian*

---

[1] French poet (1864–1936). His last two collections of poems had been *Chairs Profanes* (1889) and *Les Cornes du Faune* (1890).
[2] American artist (1863–1946). His portrait of Wilde was reproduced in *La Plume* (Paris), 15 December 1900.

*Gray* which I have told my publisher to send to you. You will find much of me in it, and, as it is cast in objective form, much that is not me. I hope you will like it, and that it will relieve the tediousness of that disappointing Atlantic! Write to me a line from New York, and believe me your affectionate friend

OSCAR WILDE

## To Stuart Merrill[1]
MS. Hyde

[*November or December 1891*] *29 Boulevard des Capucines*

Dear Stuart, I will call for you *tomorrow* at 7 o'clock. We must have a delightful evening. Ask Retté[2] to come, if you think he would like it. Ever yours OSCAR WILDE

## To Alfred Nutt[3]
MS. Private

[*November or December 1891*]  *29 Boulevard des Capucines*

Dear Mr Nutt, I enclose you a cheque for £10 on account with many thanks. I have only just received your letter or I would have answered it before.

Is there any sale for my Fairy Tales still? I think they might be run as a Christmas book. Faithfully yours

OSCAR WILDE

[1] American poet (1863–1915), who wrote in French and lived in Paris
[2] Adolphe Retté, French Symbolist poet (1863–1910). He and Merrill helped to check Wilde's French in *Salome* (see *Letters*, p. 305). In his posthumously published *Souvenirs sur le Symbolisme* (1925 but written in 1900) Merrill recorded: "*Ce ne fut pas chose facile de faire accepter à Wilde toutes mes corrections. Il écrivait le français comme il le parlait, c'est-à-dire avec une fantaisie qui, si elle était savoureuse dans la con versation, aurait produit, au théâtre, une déplorable impression.*" Merrill was also the manager of the Théâtre de l'Oeuvre in Paris where, in February 1896, *Salome* was first produced.
[3] Publisher (1856–1910). He had published *The Happy Prince* in 1888

102

## To Robert Sherard[1]
MS. Koch

[December 1891]                                         [Paris]

Dear Robert, Just enter on page one: "*Son père, Sir William Wilde, était archéologue très célèbre et homme de lettres, et du côté de sa mère il est le petit-neveu de l'étrange romancier Maturin, l'ami de Goethe, de Byron, et de Scott; l'auteur de* Melmoth, that strange and wonderful book that so thrilled Balzac and Baudelaire, and was a part of the romantic movement in France in 1830."

Also I have taken out about the guests at Tite Street. It won't do.

Do dine tonight, will you? Come at 6.30. Ever yours

OSCAR

Put "*On voyait chez lui l'élite du monde artistique,*" as I have indicated. Thanks.

---

[1] Author and journalist (1861–1943), great-grandson of Wordsworth, first met Wilde in Paris in 1883. He was still living there in 1891, and had written a long article in French on Wilde and his work, which he sent to Wilde (during his visit to Paris) for his approval. The article appeared on the front page of *Le Gaulois* on 17 December 1891. It was reprinted as an appendix to Sherard's *Oscar Wilde: the Story of an Unhappy Friendship* (privately printed, 1902). All Wilde's suggestions were incorporated in it.

# To Minna K. Gale[1]
MS. Taylor

Dear Miss Gale, I have to thank you for the very beautiful impersonation of *The Duchess of Padua* that you are presenting, and also for a charming and fascinating photograph of yourself that you have been kind enough to send me, and for which I should have before thanked you, but I have been suffering from overwork and unable to write.

I wish I could limit my letter to expressions of thanks and appreciation, but I am obliged to write to you on business also, which is as painful to me as I have no doubt it is to you.

The business matter is this: I gave you the American rights of my play because you had been the original impersonator of the Duchess, and I felt that to give the rights away from you to any other actress would be a wrong to you, and imply some doubt of your powers, of which I had no doubt, and might do you harm at the outset of your career as an actress directing your own company.

Accordingly I let you have the play on absurdly low terms, understanding also from your letter and from what my friend Mr Anderson, acting for you, told me, that my play was to be the prominent feature and basis of your tour, as Mr Barrett had purposed to make it of his. Mr Anderson told me he understood you intended playing matinées of Juliet and Beatrice, but that my play was to occupy the evening bill for most, if not all, the nights of the week.

Instead of that I find that my play is played about once a

---

[1] American actress (*c.* 1867–*c.* 1944). At the Broadway Theatre in New York she had played the Duchess of Padua to Lawrence Barrett's Guido Ferranti. Despite Wilde's mention of "a great success", its New York run lasted only three weeks. Barrett planned to take the play on tour, but he died on 20 March, so Miss Gale formed her own company for the tour. See *Letters*, p. 307.

ortnight, usually on the *last* night of your engagement in
an important place, as recently at Harlem, so that on a tour
of three months I have received royalties for eight performances!

This is of course extremely unjust to me. Had I understood that such was to be the position accorded to my play I
would not, of course, have given it to you on the very low
terms I did, or indeed given it to you at all. My play, having
been a great success in New York, should have been your
opening production at Harlem, and should have been played
during the week if the houses warranted it. To play it only
once, and on your last night, was to assign it a position it of
course does not deserve, and to rob it of its proper artistic
importance.

I understood you were to emphasise my play, to go on
tour with it as the new romantic tragedy, to assert it in each
town. I find it treated as if it was an old-fashioned, outworn
piece, to be played twice a month, and I feel deeply
wounded by the treatment it has received.

It is also a severe monetary loss to me. I fixed the royalties
ridiculously low so as not to hamper you at the outset in any
way, understanding you were starting on tour with an important, beautiful, artistic production of my play. It has not
been so. My play has been put on the shelf, and played on a
few Saturday evenings when I suppose you have had an
exhausting morning performance. You must realise that as
an artist I have not received the treatment I expected, and
was led to believe I would get. A grave injustice has been
done to me and my work.

And now, what is to be done? The present state of things
cannot go on. Will you let me have my play back? Or will
you buy my play out and out? If you like I will sell you the
*English* and American rights, provided of course that you
produce the play in London within three years. Or will you
buy the American rights alone? To be forwarded a few

105

dollars at the end of each month for my play is of course absurd and annoying.

For you personally as an actress of genius and power and beauty I have the greatest admiration. My friends tell me you realise perfectly the image put forth in the poetry and passion of my play, but had I known that my play was to be treated in the way it has been, I would of course, in justice to myself, have put it in other hands. Pray think over my letter, and let me hear from you soon. Sincerely yours

OSCAR WILDE


## To Dodd, Mead & Co[1]
MS. Hyde

[1891]                                                    16 Tite Street

Gentlemen, It will give me great pleasure to arrange with you for the publication of my book *The House of Pomegranates* in America. The edition, however, will have to be unillustrated, as the drawings and designs belong to Messrs Osgood & McIlvaine who do not wish to part with them. The stories, however, are mine and I will be happy to authorise you to publish them. My royalty will be 15 per cent on the published price.

I hope the book will be well printed and bound. I remain, gentlemen, your obedient servant          OSCAR WILDE

[1] American publishers. They took some copies of Osgood, McIlvaine' edition (1891) and published them in America early in 1892. They had already published the American edition of *Intentions* (1891).

106

## To Robert Sherard[1]
### MS. Montague

[? Early 1892]                                          Lyric Club

Dear Robert, I am so pleased you are all right. Never mind about the brute. You have asserted yourself like a brave gentleman. Ever                                          OSCAR

[1] In his 1902 volume (see note p. 103) Sherard wrote: "A few months later [than his article in *Le Gaulois*] Oscar Wilde rendered me a service for which I felt very grateful. On the eve of fighting a duel, under severe conditions, I had written to a relation of mine in London about certain arrangements in the event of my mischance. The good fellow . . . was greatly alarmed and was for informing the police . . . . However, before doing so, he went to Tite Street to consult Oscar Wilde, who . . . was able to dissuade him from an act which would have put me under *taboo* in Paris for the rest of my days. And after the business was over I received a letter from Wilde . . . . He knew the circumstances, and he wrote to approve of my conduct. I do not think that any of his letters ever gave me so much pleasure."

There is no proof, but a strong supposition, that this is that letter. For Sherard's account of the duel see his *My Friends the French* (1910).

# To John Barlas[1]
MS. Hyde

[Postmark 19 January 1892]                    *16 Tite Street*

My dear friend and poet, Thanks, a thousand thanks, for your charming letter. Whatever I did was merely what you would have done for me or for any friend of yours whom you admired and appreciated. We poets and dreamers are all brothers.

I am so glad you are feeling better. I now know nerves myself, what they are, and what rest can do for them. We will have many days of song and joy together when the spring comes, and life shall be made lovely for us, and we will pipe on reeds. I must come and see you soon. Your affectionate friend                    OSCAR

---

[1] Scottish poet and revolutionary Socialist (1860–1914). Friend of William Morris. Married a grand-niece of Nelson and had a son. Published eight volumes of verse between 1884 and 1893. On "Bloody Sunday" (13 November 1887) he took part in the riot in Trafalgar Square, after which he and Cunninghame Graham were arrested and imprisoned. Barlas received a severe blow on the head from a policeman's truncheon, which affected his reason. On 31 December 1891 he discharged the contents of a revolver outside the Speaker's House in the Palace of Westminster, saying: "I am an anarchist. What I have done is to show my contempt for the House of Commons." After a remand in custody, and a medical report saying he was not in his right mind, on 16 January 1892 he was bound over to keep the peace in the sum of £200. Half of this was guaranteed by Wilde and half by Henry Hyde Champion (1859–1928), soldier, journalist, publisher and Socialist, whose firm The Modern Press had published Bernard Shaw's first novel *Cashel Byron's Profession* in 1886. This letter is clearly in answer to Barlas's letter of gratitude. He died in a lunatic asylum.

## To John Barlas
MS. Hyde

[*Postmark 4 February 1892*]                    *16 Tite Street*

My dear poet, With great pleasure. Have I a form to fill up?[1]
Or is a letter what is necessary? In all things command me.

The question of the "particular purpose". Only your wish
to read in a public museum is a general question addressed
to all, as many illiterate persons seek admission, whose sole
object is either to read the *Family Herald*, or to write it,
which is worse.

Send me a line, poet and scholar, and know me for ever
your friend                                        OSCAR


## To George Alexander[2]
MS. Hyde

[*Mid-February 1892*]                          *16 Tite Street*

Dear Aleck, I heard by chance in the theatre today — after
you had left the stage — that you intended using the first
scene a second time — in the last act. I think you should
have told me this, as after a long consultation on the subject
more than four weeks ago you agreed to have what is
directed in the book of the play, namely Lady Windermere's
boudoir, a scene which I consider very essential from a
dramatic point of view.

My object, however, in writing is not to reproach you in
any way — reproaches being useless things — but to point

---

[1] Presumably for admission to the Reading Room of the British Museum.
[2] Actor-manager (1858–1918). Knighted 1911. *Lady Windermere's Fan*
was first produced at the St James's Theatre on 20 February 1892, with
Alexander as Lord Windermere and Marion Terry as Mrs Erlynne.

this out. If through pressure of time, or for reasons of economy, you are unable to give the play its full scenic mounting, the scene that has to be repeated should be *the second, not the first*. Lady Windermere *may* be in her drawing-room in the fourth act. *She should not be in her husband's library*. This is a very important point.

Now, from the point of view of stage-management, the advantages of using Scene II are these:

In Act 2 the scene is night. The ballroom is open, and so is the terrace. In Act 4, the scene being day, the ballroom is closed, the window shut, and the furniture can be differently arranged. Rooms are cleared out of some of their contents for a reception. These contents are restored the next day. That is to say, the repetition of the library would have to be an exact replica: the repetition of the drawing-room would not have this disadvantage.

And the disadvantage is a great one, because the scene — a vital one in the play — between the Duchess and Lady Windermere takes place on the sofa on the right of the stage. Now Mrs Erlynne should not have her scene in the same place. It impoverishes the effect. I want you to arrange Mrs Erlynne on a sofa more in the centre of the stage and towards the left side. In my own rough draft of the stage-setting of this act, made when I was writing the piece, I placed Mrs Erlynne on a high-backed Louis Seize sofa so:

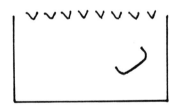

She would then be, what she should be, in full view of the audience. She should not be at the side. The situation is too important. The sofa is of course not parallel with the foot-

110

lights. It is placed like this ⟩⌣ and Mrs Erlynne sits on the upper side naturally. Will you kindly think very seriously over this. The use of the second act, instead of the first, enables us to give Mrs Erlynne a very much better position on the stage. There are only three people in the last act (setting aside the servants) till the arrival of Lord Augustus, and the play should not go on in a corner. Mrs Erlynne should hold the centre of the stage, and be its central figure.

This also is to be remembered. Windermere, being in his own house, can pace up and down — does, in fact, do so; Mrs Erlynne, of course, cannot do anything of the kind. She rises from the sofa, as marked in the play, and sits down, but with the possibility of Lady Windermere entering at any moment, for her to walk about, or cross, or the like, would be melodramatic, but not dramatic or artistic.

All this, of such importance to the play, I should have liked to have talked over with you personally, but, in spite of my earnest request to you conveyed in my letter of some days ago, you have not given me what I wanted, and what my position, as the creator of the play, entitles me to, and that is a formal quiet interview with you at the end of each day's rehearsal. In the interests of the play, that should be done. It saves a great trouble. It would in the present instance have saved me writing this long letter, the points of which could have been more easily put forward in conversation, when I would also have had the advantage of hearing your own views on the many points.

One last point. When Windermere says, on Mrs Erlynne's exit, "Allow me", he goes to the door. His wife on Mrs Erlynne's exit goes towards him, and I want you both to get to the *back of the stage*. Lord Augustus enters below you, takes you by arm to the front of stage. Lady Windermere watches from the back, till her anxiety becomes unbearable, and then comes down. It is essential that Lady Windermere

111

should not hear one word of Lord Augustus's account of Mrs Erlynne's explanation.

Pray give your serious attention to all these points, and believe me very sincerely yours          OSCAR WILDE

## *To George Alexander*
MS. Texas

[*Mid-February 1892*]                                    *Hotel Albemarle*

Dear Alexander, I am too unwell to attend rehearsal this morning. If there is one this evening I will come. Perhaps Mr Shone[1] will kindly let me know. In any case I hope that there will be no repetition of the painful scene of last night. I have always treated you with personal courtesy, and I expect to be treated with equal courtesy in return.

And now, about the play. Will you kindly consider these points. Details in life are of no importance, but in art details are vital.

In the comedy scenes people should speak out more, be more assertive. Every *word* of a comedy dialogue should reach the ears of the audience. This applies specially to the Duchess, who should be larger in assertion. The chatter that drowned her speech in *Act 2* about Mrs Erlynne and the Savile girls might be *before* her entrance, and the guests pass chattering on to the terrace, leaving two on the sofa at back, and two on the seat at entrance.

Hopper had better have either his own hair or a quiet wig. His face last night was far too white, and his appearance

[1] R.V. Shone, business manager of the St James's Theatre.

far too ridiculous. Personally I think his own hair, and his face made up younger than it is naturally.

Last night, whether by inadvertence or direction I don't know, the Duchess left out some essential words in her first speech to Hopper. It should run, ". . . kangaroos flying about. *Agatha has found Australia on the map. What a curious shape it is!* However, it's a very young country, isn't it?"

The words she left out are those I have underlined. They give the point to the remark about the young country. To omit them is to leave out the point of the climax, and in point of time nothing is saved by their omission. The words take less than ten seconds to speak.

I think also that C. Graham should not take his aunt into the ballroom — young dandies dislike their aged relatives — at least rarely pay them attention. Lady J. should have a debutante in tow, and Mrs Erlynne might give the speech about Dumby to Graham, and then turn to you.

With regard to yourself, when Cecil Graham bores you with his chatter you broke off last night by saying "How amusing!", or some word like that. I think it would be better to say "Excuse me for a moment", as I suggested. Lord W. is terribly agitated about Mrs Erlynne's coming, and the dandy's chatter bores him, does not please him. He has no taste for it.

Also, on going on to the terrace with Mrs Erlynne, last night you said "Come on to the terrace." Now Lord W. is not anxious to keep Mrs Erlynne in his house. She forces him to do what she wants. Let her say, "Let us go on to the terrace." He, cold and somewhat disdainful, though that is too strong a word, has to do her will.

Will you kindly think over these two points.

Also, would you remind Lady Plymdale to say "That woman!" not "That *dreadful* woman." We must not make Mrs E. look like a cocotte. She is an adventuress, not a cocotte.

113

I hope everything is going right. It seemed to me that only the details wanted finishing. Yours truly

OSCAR WILDE

Act 3. Lord A's coat is too horsy: also he should take it off. He wants to make a night of it.

I write from bed which accounts for pencil.

## To Arthur Clifton
MS. Jestin

[Postmark 17 February 1892]                    Hotel Albemarle

Dear Arthur, I hope you will come to my first night in my wife's box. You could be of great service to her as she will be very nervous probably, and it would be nice for her to have an old friend with her. Her aunt Mrs William Napier[1] accompanies her.

I have been very ill, and the drains at Tite Street have gone wrong, so we have all separated — Constance and Vyvyan, who is ill, to Lady Mount-Temple's,[2] Cyril to Mrs Napier's, myself to a quiet room here. Ever yours   OSCAR

Box D, but wait in vestibule for them like a good boy.

---

[1] Louisa Mary Lloyd married (1854) William Napier, second son of the ninth Lord Napier. She died in 1908.
[2] Georgina Tollemache (1822–1901), widow of the First Lord Mount-Temple (1811–88). She was a distant cousin of Constance Wilde and was unfailingly kind to her and her children.

## To an Unidentified Editor
MS. Cleveland

*16 Tite Street*

Sir, John is an admirable name. It was the name of the most charming of all the Disciples, the one who did not write the Fourth Gospel. It was the name of the most perfect of all the English poets of this century, as it was of the greatest English poet of all the centuries. Popes and Princes, wicked or wonderful, have been called John. John has been the name of several eminent journalists and criminals. But John is not amongst the many delightful names given to me at my baptism. So kindly let me correct the statement made by your reckless dramatic critic in his last and unavailing attack on my play. The attempt he makes to falsify one of the most important facts in the History of Art must be checked at once. I remain sir your obedient servant   OSCAR WILDE


## To Mrs W.H. Grenfell
MS. Grenfell

[*Postmark 3 May 1892*]                                   *16 Tite Street*

Dear Mrs Grenfell, I am quite unhappy to think that a letter from you should have met the fate of the Israelites[1] in the Red Sea, for it never reached me, and I want it. You must write it over again, or repeat it to me, or invent another to take its place. Perhaps it would be better to repeat it, so pray let me know when you come to town, and ask me to tea. It is ages since we met.

From your unkind quotation from *Lady Windermere's Fan* I discern you have been to the St James's. I wish I had

---

[1] Wilde must have meant Egyptians.

been there the same night. Shall we make up a party and go? In any case let me know when you come to town. Sincerely yours                                    OSCAR WILDE

How excellent W.H.G.'s paper in the *Nineteenth Century* is. I was delighted to see it.[1]


## To the Hon. George Curzon
### MS. Curzon

*[14 June 1892]*[2]

My dear George, On Thursday at 8 o'clock with great pleasure. Ever yours                                    OSCAR WILDE


## To Elkin Mathews[3]
### MS. Clark

*[Mid-June 1892]*                          *The Bodley Head, Vigo Street*

Dear Mr Mathews, In your estimate of the "first charges" on the book[4] you include *"advertising"*: now advertising seems to me too indefinite a thing. There is no limit to it at all, nor was it mentioned in our talk. It does not seem to me to be practical. As for the price, that had better not be settled till the book is bound — we will see then how it looks. Kindly let me hear from you on this matter. Truly yours                                    OSCAR WILDE


[1] "Lost in the Rockies" by W.H. Grenfell in the May 1892 issue.
[2] So dated by recipient.
[3] Publisher and bookseller (1851–1921). Since 1887 he had been a partner of John Lane (1854–1925) in the Bodley Head.
[4] John Gray's *Silverpoints.*

## Mathews and Lane to Wilde
MS. Princeton

*17 June 1892*                                          *Vigo Street*

Dear Sir, *Silverpoints* (poems) by John Gray. We agree to
issue the above book in the autumn on your undertaking the
cost of the designs — block for same — paper, printing and
binding of an edition not exceeding 250 copies.

In advertising the above, at your charge, we undertake
not to exceed the sum of £7.10.0, which sum shall also
include the cost of the prospectus.

We deduct a commission of 40% on the published price of
each copy sold, for our part as publishers, out of which we
make the usual trade allowances.

ELKIN MATHEWS AND JOHN LANE

I agree to the above.                         OSCAR WILDE


## To Elkin Mathews
MS. Hyde

*[Early July 1892]*
           *51 Kaiser-Friedrich's Promenade, Bad-Homburg*

Dear Mr Mathews, I enclose agreement for Mr Gray's
poems. Will you let me have agreement for *Sphinx*. I was so
busy before leaving town I could not call. Sincerely yours
                                              OSCAR WILDE

# To Herbert Beerbohm Tree[1]

My dear Tree, I hereby agree to assign you the rights in my play entitled *A Woman of No Importance* for performance in Great Britain and Ireland, on condition that you produce it at the Haymarket Theatre after *Hypatia*[2] (reserving to yourself the right to interpose revival) and pay me the following fees: when the gross receipts for six performances are under £600 you shall pay me nothing, when the gross weekly receipts are over £600 and under £800 you shall pay me 6%, when the gross weekly receipts are over £800 and under £1000 you shall pay me 7½%, and when the gross weekly receipts are over £1000 you shall pay me 10% of such gross receipts, it being understood that the sums stated are in each case for six performances and that £100 shall be added to such sums for seven or eight or more performances.

In the provinces of Great Britain and Ireland, the said play shall be our joint property, but if you elect to play it yourself in the provinces you shall pay me 5% of the gross receipts.                                        OSCAR WILDE

---

[1] Actor-manager (1853–1917). Text from a typed copy in the files of Messrs Parker Garrett & Co. At the top is written, presumably by the lawyer, "Copy of original stamped agreement", and at the bottom is typed the date of receipt, 14 October 1892.
[2] A play by G. Stuart Ogilvie, based on Charles Kingsley's novel.

# To Elisabeth Marbury[1]
## MS. NYPL

[*February 1893*]                                   *16 Tite Street*

Dear Miss Marbury, I hope you like the play, and that Frohman[2] also is pleased with it. The real title as I wired to you is *A Woman of No Importance*. There are some cuts to be made, and I don't know if the Americans, a sensitive, over-sensitive people, will be annoyed at some foolish good-natured badinage about their country in the second act. If so, and you would know better than I do, we could cut there: the lines are merely light comedy lines of no particular value, except to Lord Illingworth.

I am much obliged to you for the press-cuttings: the play[3] seems to have been a great success: but I thought Frohman was going to have *his own* production in New York: I see it's Mr Palmer's company who are to play.[4] I hear Barrymore dresses the part badly, and does not see that Darlington is *not* a villain, but a man who really believes that Windermere is treating his wife badly, and wishes to save her. His appeal is not to the weakness, but to the strength of her character (Act II): in Act III his words show he really loves her.

Am I wrong in supposing Frohman intended a production of his own in New York?

With regard to new play, it would be better to produce it in the autumn, would it not? after the Haymarket produc-

[1] New York play agent (1856–1933). She handled the American rights of all Wilde's plays from 1893.
[2] Charles Frohman, American impresario (1860–1915). Drowned in the *Lusitania*.
[3] *Lady Windermere's Fan*.
[4] It was not Frohman who produced *Lady Windermere's Fan* in America, but Albert Marshman Palmer (1838–1905). It opened at Boston on 23 January 1893 and in New York on 6 February. Maurice Barrymore (father of Ethel, John, and Lionel) played Lord Darlington.

tion is in full swing. I would not like it produced before, as the ultimate version must be the version produced under the direct supervision of the author. I need not tell you, with your experience and artistic instinct, how a play grows at rehearsal, and what new points one can introduce. Besides, it would damage my London production, and I have promised Tree that he shall have the first production: it is to be produced after *Hypatia* — I expect in April next, but don't know.[1]

With regard to the parts: Lady Stutfield is very serious and romantic — she must play as if she was playing the heroine of a romance. Lady Hunstanton is genial, loveable, and kind: Lady Caroline hard and bitter: the girl simple and direct: the boy must be charming and young: as for the mother, Agnes Booth[2] must play it. Lord Illingworth requires great distinction: the finest touch and style. If Frohman won't have the play, you must get Palmer to do it: and make great terms. With many thanks, believe me your sincere friend and admirer          OSCAR WILDE

## *To Richard Le Gallienne*[3]
### MS. Clark

*[22 or 23 February 1893]*          *Babbacombe Cliff*

My dear Richard, I have just read the *Star*, and write to tell you how pleased I am that you, with your fluid artistic temperament, should have glided into the secret of the soul

---

[1] *Hypatia* finished at the Haymarket Theatre on 13 April 1893, and *A Woman of No Importance* opened there on 19 April.
[2] Australian-born actress (1846–1910).
[3] His review of the original (French) edition of *Salome* appeared, signed LOGROLLER, in the *Star* of 22 February 1893, where it occupied twenty-eight and a half single-column inches of praise and description, including the prophetic words "It seems built to music. Its gradual growth is exactly like the development of a theme in music."

of my poem, swiftly, surely, just as years ago you glided into my heart.

There are of course things I regret, for yourself. Journalism is a terrible cave where the divine become tainted — for a moment only. Why should the young prophet, rising from the well of darkness, be like a "jack in the box"? Why is it that you describe the chill, sceptical, rationalistic Herodias as an "unimaginative worldly creature"? She is far more than that: she is reason in its tragic raiment, reason with its tragic end — and, oh! Richard, why say I am amusing, when Herod hears that in his *royaume* there is one who can make the dead come to life, and (filled with terror at so hideous a prospect) says in his insolence and his fear "That I do not allow". "It would be terrible if the dead came back."

But nothing matters much. You have got into the secret chamber of the house in which *Salome* was fashioned, and I rejoice to think that to you has my secret been revealed, for you are the lover of beauty, and by her much — perhaps over-much — loved and worshipped. Ever yours    OSCAR

## *To Bertram Grosvenor Goodhue*[1]
### MS. Clark

[*June 1893*]                                        *16 Tite Street*

Dear Sir, It would give me great pleasure to have an edition of *A House of Pomegranates* brought out by your artistic and distinguished firm, whose work I have often admired.

I think it would be better to omit the illustrations, lovely

[1] 1869–1924. Partner in the publishing firm of Copeland & Day in Boston, Mass. Goodhue answered favourably on 28 June, but Copeland & Day did not publish *A House of Pomegranates* (originally published by Osgood, McIlvaine in 1891), though they did publish American editions of the English translation of *Salome* (1894) and of *The Sphinx* (1894).

as they are. You might have a few headpieces and initial letters and *culs-de-lampe* for the divisions of "The Fisherman and his Soul", where I have placed pomegranates.

Would you like to print my story on Shakespeare's sonnets — appearing here in October (Mathews & Lane)? If so I will send you proofs.[1] The terms you offer seem to me quite fair.

The copyright of *A House of Pomegranates* is my own — so far as I have any copyright. Truly yours

OSCAR WILDE

## Cable to Rose Coghlan[2]
MS. Koch

[*Autumn 1893*]

Hope you will be able to get Elsie de Wolfe[3] for comedy part in my play. She would be very good.    OSCAR WILDE

## Cable to Elisabeth Marbury
MS. Koch

[*Autumn 1893*]

Have wired Coghlan to secure Elsie de Wolfe.    WILDE

[1] The enlarged version of *The Portrait of Mr W.H.*, which was not published until 1921 in America and 1958 in England.

[2] English actress (1851–1932) who worked mostly in America. On 11 December 1893 she presented *A Woman of No Importance* at the Fifth Avenue Theatre in New York, with herself and Maurice Barrymore in leading parts.

[3] American society woman (1865–1950). Bosom-friend and lifelong companion of Elisabeth Marbury. Elsie was at this time a promising amateur actress, but she was given no part in Wilde's play. Later she became internationally known as an interior decorator. In 1926 she married Sir Charles Mendl (1871–1958), Press Attaché at the British Embassy in Paris, where she became even better known as Lady Mendl.

Both these cables are in Wilde's hand on one sheet of paper, and were presumably later transferred to post-office forms.

## To Charles Ricketts[1]

*[Spring 1894]*

I return proofs corrected.[2] Don't you think the pages are terribly few in number? Why not put fewer verses on each page? We could easily have four or five pages more . . . . I want you not to allow Lane to have any advertisement pages in the book; silly things about Le Gallienne are out of place in a work of art.

## To Leo Maxse[3]
MS. Chichester

*[c. 1894]*                                                    *16 Tite Street*

Dear Sir, I never write "slashing" articles: slash does not seem to me to be a quality of good prose. Still less would I feel inclined to write an article attacking all that is known by the term *"Fin-de-Siècle"*.

All that is known by that term I particularly admire and love. It is the fine flower of our civilisation: the only thing that keeps the world from the commonplace, the coarse, the barbarous.

But perhaps your letter was intended for someone else. It seems to me to be addressed to a journalist, not to an artist. However, I merely judge by internal evidence. Faithfully yours                                          OSCAR WILDE

[1] Artist, writer, book and stage designer (1866–1931). He designed or decorated a number of Wilde's books. Text of this fragment from the *Autograph*, Vol 1, No 5, May 1912.
[2] Presumably the corrected proofs of *The Sphinx*, which Wilde had asked for (*Letters*, p. 341). The book was published, with decorations by Ricketts, on 11 June 1894. It consisted of forty-four pages, six of them blank.
[3] Leopold James Maxse (1864–1932), diehard Tory journalist and political writer. Editor of the *National Review* from 1893.

## To John Lane[1]

*[August 1894]*                    *5 Esplanade, Worthing*

I return corrected proofs.[2] The title-page, dedication, play-
bill etc. have not yet come . . . . I wish the reader would go
through the play once and correct any slips in the use of
"will" and "shall" — my use of the words is Celtic not
Saxon . . . . I think the plays had better remain with Mr
Lane, at Bodley Head, as they form a series that should not
be broken.[3] Mr Mathews might have *The Portrait of Mr
W.H.* and that would give an opportunity of making some
alterations in the usual issue and price. 300 or 250, and 50
large-paper would be better. Also the book should be a
guinea. These, at least, are Mr Ricketts's views. This book
should be out by the end of October. I have to get *A
Woman of No Importance* copyrighted simultaneously in
America (please mark copyright as in *Lady Windermere's
Fan*. This is most important) . . . I think the book can be out
. . . when the play goes on tour . . . should have a good sale
at Liverpool where it has been lectured on and formed a text
for reckless sermons.

## John Lane to Wilde
MS. Clark

*7 September 1894*                              *G1 The Albany*[4]

Dear Mr Wilde, Mr Mathews, it appears, has had some
correspondence with you re the distribution of your books

[1] Text from the Dulau Catalogue of Books from the Library of John
Lane (1929).
[2] Of *A Woman of No Importance.*
[3] The partnership between Lane and Mathews was dissolved in August
1894.
[4] The office of the Bodley Head.

on our dissolving partnership. You wrote quite frankly to the firm that you wished me to retain the plays and that you wished Mr Mathews to publish *Mr W.H.* I was perfectly agreeable to that arrangement, but it now appears that Mr Mathews has again communicated with you on the subject and he declines to have *Mr W.H.* at "any price," but he wants the plays. Since I have pointed out that if he takes the plays he must also take *Mr W.H.* he declines both.

For my part I am perfectly willing to publish your plays and *Mr W.H.* provided I see and approve the latter before it is printed, but I am sure that you as a man of the world would not expect me or any other publisher to issue a book he had never seen.

Can we not meet, talk the matter over and settle things? Yours very truly                          JOHN LANE[1]


## The Bodley Head to Wilde
### Draft in Clark

*21 September 1894*

Dear Sir, We have considered your letter in all its bearings and have come to the following decision.

Mr Lane will carry out the firm's agreement with you with regard to your three plays, *Salome* and *The Sphinx*. As to *Mr W.H.* we are agreed that Mr Lane shall accept all responsibilities assumed by the firm in the agreement. There can be no grounds however for your complaint against the firm with regard to the lapse of time since the agreement for this book was entered upon, as we have never received the manuscript. If you will send it to Mr Lane he is prepared to deal with it immediately.[2]

[1] For Wilde's answer to this letter, agreeing to Lane's proposal, see *Letters*, pp. 365–6.
[2] For Wilde's long answer to this letter, see *Letters*, pp. 367–8.

## To Elkin Mathews & John Lane

MS. Taylor

[*Late September 1894*]                    *5 Esplanade, Worthing*

Gentlemen, I enclose you a telegram I have received from New York to announce the copyright of my play at last.[1] I suppose the English edition is quite ready, so pray announce it at once. The play itself is now being performed at *Liverpool*, and will go on to Glasgow, Edinburgh, Newcastle, Birmingham etc.

You might send some copies to these towns, especially *Liverpool*. Also copies should be sent to the chief paper of each of these towns: one paper in each would be enough. In London kindly send *no* copy to the *Sunday Sun* or the *Daily Sun*. It would merely result in some new impertinence by O'Connor, who, I hear, is deeply mortified by my *exposé* of his conduct.[2] The *Saturday Review*, the *Academy*, and the *Athenaeum* might be left out also: this, however, is a matter for you.

How about the *édition de luxe* of *The Sphinx*?[3] I have had no copy. Yours faithfully                    OSCAR WILDE

[1] *A Woman of No Importance*, which Lane published on 9 October 1894. A provincial touring company headed by Lewis Waller performed the play at the Shakespeare Theatre, Liverpool, from 24 to 29 September.
[2] T.P. O'Connor (1848–1929), journalist and politician, was the founder and first editor of the *Star*, the *Sun*, the *Sunday Sun*, and *T.P.'s Weekly*. On 5 August 1894 the *Sunday Sun* published some doggerel verses over Wilde's name. After being convinced that Wilde had not written the lines, O'Connor, in the same paper, accused him of having plagiarised them. Wilde replied at length in the *Pall Mall Gazette* of 18 and 22 September (see *Letters*, pp. 370–72).
[3] The ordinary edition of *The Sphinx* (250 copies at two guineas) had been published by Mathews & Lane on 11 June 1894. The twenty-five copies on large paper appeared later in the year.

# To John Lane[1]

[c. late September 1894]      *Office of The Yellow Book*[2]

Dear Mr Lane, I think we must really settle this question of *Mr W.H.* before we proceed to our other schemes. If Ricketts cannot do it, surely there is someone else who can design a dainty book. Nutt tells me that his average yearly sale of *The Happy Prince* is about 150! This is really absurd. Truly yours                    OSCAR WILDE

# To Fred Terry[3]

*[c. December 1894]*                    *16 Tite Street*

Morell[4] writes to me that your charming wife is a little afraid that the part of Lady Chiltern in my play is not the best part of the female characters. Let me assure you that it is what I believe is called the part of the "leading lady": it is the important part, and the only sympathetic part. Indeed the other woman does not appear in the last act at all.

I am greatly pleased that I have the good fortune to have your wife in the cast, and on her much of the fortune of the play will depend.[5] Truly yours                    OSCAR WILDE

---

[1] Text from Seven Gables Bookshop, New York, and Dulau catalogue.
[2] The first of the thirteen volumes of this periodical, published by Lane, appeared on 16 April 1894. Wilde was never a contributor.
[3] Actor brother of Ellen (1863–1933). He had played the part of Gerald Arbuthnot in *A Woman of No Importance*. Text from an auction catalogue, where the last paragraph is reproduced in facsimile.
[4] H.H. Morell (1865–1916) presented *An Ideal Husband* in partnership with Lewis Waller, who played the leading rôle.
[5] Julia Neilson (1867–1957), who married Fred Terry in 1891, had played the part of Hester Worsley in *A Woman of No Importance*, and duly appeared as Lady Chiltern when *An Ideal Husband* opened at the Theatre Royal, Haymarket, on 3 January 1895. The play was withdrawn on 6 April.

## To William Heinemann[1]
### MS. Burgunder

[*? c. 2 January 1895*]                    *Hotel Albemarle*

Dear Mr Heinemann, What an eleventh hour to come at! I have had very few seats at my disposal, and have only one left. However, I know your real interest in literature, and send it to you enclosed, with real pleasure. Truly yours

OSCAR WILDE


## To Robert Ross
### MS. Private

[*c. 25 January 1895*[2]]              *Hôtel de l'Europe, Algiers*

Dearest Bobbie, Thank you so much. The interview is most brilliant and delightful,[3] and your forwarding my letters really most sweet of you.

There is a great deal of beauty here. The Kabyle boys are quite lovely. At first we had some difficulty in procuring a proper civilised guide. But now it is all right, and Bosie and I have taken to haschish: it is quite exquisite: three puffs of smoke and then peace and love. Bosie wakes up at night and cries like a child for the best haschish.

---

[1] English publisher (1863–1920). Founded his own firm 1890. He had published a paperback edition of *Intentions* in his English Library at Leipzig in October 1891.

[2] Wilde and Lord Alfred (Bosie) Douglas arrived at Algiers on 17 January, and Wilde left on 31 January. They ran into André Gide at Blidah on 27 January. This is the first letter known to have survived from Algiers, and it may be the only one Wilde wrote there.

[3] "Mr Oscar Wilde on Mr Oscar Wilde; An Interview", which appeared anonymously in the *St James's Gazette* on 18 January 1895. Some have assumed that it was entirely written by Wilde, but his words in this letter make me believe that the interview was a collaboration between him and Ross. It is here printed as Appendix A. on pp. 189–96.

We have been an excursion into the mountains of Kabylia
— full of villages peopled by fauns. Several shepherds
fluted on reeds for us. We were followed by lovely brown
things from forest to forest. The beggars here have profiles,
so the problem of poverty is easily solved.

You are a great dear over my letters. Bosie sends his love,
so do I. Ever yours                                         OSCAR

The most beautiful boy in Algiers is said by the guide to be
"deceitful": isn't it sad? Bosie and I are awfully upset
about it.


## To an Unidentified Correspondent[1]
### MS. Hyde

*[14 February 1895]*

Bosie's father[2] is going to make a scene tonight. I am going
to stop him.


## C.O. Humphreys, Son, & Kershaw[3] to Wilde
### MS. Clark

*28 February 1895      Giltspur Chambers, Holborn Viaduct* ·

Dear Sir
### In re The Marquis of Queensberry
We regret that we are unable to carry out your instruc-
tions to prosecute the Marquis of Queensberry for his
threats and insulting conduct towards you on the 14th

---

1 Almost certainly Robbie Ross.
2 The ninth Marquess of Queensberry (1844–1900).
3 Solicitors who acted for Wilde throughout his trials.

instant at the St James's Theatre[1] inasmuch as upon investigating the case we have met with every obstruction from Mr George Alexander, the manager, and his staff at the theatre, who decline to give us any statements or to render any assistance to you in your desire to prosecute Lord Queensberry and without whose evidence and assistance we cannot advise you to venture upon a prosecution. You personally would of course be unable to give evidence of that which occurred behind your back as to which you have no personal knowledge beyond information from others who apprised you of the insulting threats and conduct of his Lordship.

Had Lord Queensberry been permitted to carry out his threats you would have had ample ground for instituting a prosecution against him, but the only consolation we can offer to you now is that such a persistent persecutor as Lord Queensberry will probably give you another opportunity sooner or later of seeking the protection of the Law, in which event we shall be happy to render you every assistance in our power to bring him to justice and thus secure to you future peace at his hands. We are, dear sir, yours faithfully
C.O. HUMPHREYS, SON, & KERSHAW

[1] On the first night of *The Importance of Being Earnest* (14 February 1895) Lord Queensberry was prevented from entering the theatre, where he planned to address the audience, and had to content himself by prowling round the theatre with a prize-fighter and leaving a bouquet of vegetables at the stage-door.

# READING

1895-97

# To an Unidentified Correspondent[1]
## MS. Hyde

*15 April 1895*                    *H.M. Prison, Holloway*

My dear kind good sweet friend, What can I say to you? How can I thank you? I cannot express anything adequately. I am dazed with horror. Life has at last become to me as real as a dream.

What more hideous things may crawl out to cry against me I don't know. I hardly care, I think, for sometimes there is sunlight in my cell, and every day someone whose name is Love comes to see me, and weeps so much through prison-bars that it is I who have to comfort him.[2]

With my deepest affection, my most sincere gratitude, ever yours                                   OSCAR


# To Messrs Stoker & Hansell[3]

*31 December 1896*                    *H.M. Prison, Reading*

Gentlemen, I hereby authorize you to act as my solicitors in reference to my family affairs, both with regard to my life interest in my wife's estate, and also to the guardianship of my children, and I request you to inform Messrs Hargrove & Son, 16 Victoria Street, Westminster Abbey, S.W.,[4] that I desire that any communication which they

---

[1] Perhaps Adela Schuster, who had given Wilde £1000, or Mrs Bernard Beere, to whom he had sent gratitude in his letter to Adey and Ross of 9 April 1895 (*Letters*, p. 390). If it had been Ada Leverson she would certainly have included it in *Letters to the Sphinx from Oscar Wilde* (1930).
[2] Lord Alfred Douglas.
[3] From a copy in a clerkly hand in the Hyde collection.
[4] The solicitors of Constance Wilde's family.

may have to make to me should be made to me through you.

I believe I am correct in stating that the general outlines of the matter at issue have been communicated, by or through Mr More Adey,[1] to you, but I am anxious, for your guidance and satisfaction, as well as for my own, that my own wishes and views should be clearly conveyed to you under my own hand.

I feel that it is quite right that the guardianship of the children should be vested in my wife, and that she should have the right to appoint guardians for them in case of her decease. In the latter case I think I should be allowed access to them "at reasonable intervals on occasions approved of by the guardians". In the former case I would be ready to leave the matter to my wife, and to engage not to make any attempt to see the children against her wishes, or to communicate with them in any way except through her. I agree readily to their bearing another name than mine: the name, in fact, she has chosen which is an old family name on her side. I would not myself wish to reside in the same town with them. I propose to live, if I live anywhere, in Brussels. I have written all this to my wife, and I have also conveyed it to Mr Hargrove.

With regard to money affairs, the offer made to me by my wife of £150 a year is, of course, extremely small. I certainly hoped that £200 would have been fixed on. I understand that my wife alleges as one of the reasons for £150 being selected that she wishes to pay off a debt of £500 due from me to her brother Mr Otho Lloyd, at the rate of £50 a year. I think, with Mr Adey, that I should have the £200 if that debt should be paid off by me. However, I do not wish to haggle over the terms, though of course I think them small. The income under our marriage settlement is about £1000

---

[1] William More Adey (1858–1942), close friend of Robbie Ross.

a year, and on the death of Mrs Wilde's mother some addition will accrue.

With regard to my life interest I sincerely hope that half at least will be purchased for me. My wife does not realise that in case of my surviving her and living to any advanced age it would really be bad for my children to have an unfortunate father living in penury, and perhaps forced to make application for assistance to them. Such a state of things would be in every way undesirable and unseemly. In the case of my surviving my wife I wish to be placed above any necessity of troubling my children for my support. I was in hopes that at least half the interest would by this time have been secured, but I have been misled by Mr Hargrove's letter, which I enclose. As regards the other half, if it also could be got for me it would enable me to resettle it at once on the children as a proof of the affection I have for them and the genuineness of the position I am taking up with regard to their future welfare.

I should mention that my wife came to see me at Wandsworth prison and wrote to me a very touching and affectionate letter then (October year last[1]). She also on the death of my mother, Lady Wilde, came to break the news to me here in person[2] and displayed great tenderness and affection, but it is now nearly a year since I have seen her, and the long absence, combined with influences hostile to me personally surrounding her, has made her take up a certain stand with regard to my life interest and my income during her life. She is quite aware of the deep affection existing between me and my sons, and in her last letter (November 21) expresses her hope that "when they are older they may be proud to acknowledge me as their father" and that I may win back the intellectual position I have lost; with other gracious

[1] Actually 21 September.
[2] On 19 February 1896. She had travelled all the way from Genoa.

wishes. Mr Hargrove in one of his letters stated that the proposed £150 a year would be forfeited on my breaking any of the conditions attached to it. This is, I admit, a painful and humiliating position for me to look forward to. I think my solemn agreement should be sufficient. The happiness of my children is my sole object and desire.

Would you kindly ask Mr More Adey to use all his efforts to see me here *himself*. I have much to talk to him about. Also tell him that I *quite* understand that the books were a present from my friend Mr Humphreys the publisher.[1] Also that Mr Alexander holds no French rights at all in *Lady Windermere's Fan* (one of my comedies) but that I am glad he should act for me.

I hope you will allow me to express in conclusion my thanks to you for undertaking this delicate and difficult matter for me. It relieves me of a great deal of the mental anxiety and distress incident on my condition, and intensified by Mr Hargrove's violent and harsh letters. I remain yours faithfully                                                   OSCAR WILDE


## To A.D. Hansell[2]

*12 April 1897*                              [*H.M. Prison, Reading*]

Dear Sir, I have to acknowledge the receipt of your letter of the 10th which the Governor has kindly handed to me, and I am very much relieved and indeed pleased by the turn affairs have taken. I am quite satisfied with the arrange-

---

[1] Arthur L. Humphreys, bookseller, author and publisher (1865–1946). For many years head of Hatchard's bookshop in Piccadilly. In January 1895 he produced fifty copies of *Oscariana*, a collection of epigrams from Wilde's work chosen by Constance Wilde, and in May a further edition of 200. In May 1895 he issued a privately printed edition (50 copies) of Wilde's *The Soul of Man under Socialism*. Constance became very fond of him.

[2] Text from a copy in More Adey's hand in the Clark collection.

ment, and hope that your position as arbiter of my conduct will not be an onerous one. Will you kindly convey to my wife's solicitors my acceptance of the terms proposed. I suppose some deed requiring my signature will have to be drawn up by them? I should prefer to sign this on my release, if my signing it here would involve my being described as "residing in Reading Gaol", an address, which, however admirable from an ethical point of view, will not, I trust, be permanent in character; in any case there is no need to have it in family deeds. If my address can be given *pro forma* elsewhere, I should be charmed to sign anything here as it would give me the pleasure of another visit from you.

I suppose my wife will repay the £75 already paid for my share in my marriage settlement? This would only be right. If the subject has not been mentioned, would you state to Mr Hargrove that I certainly would expect it. I do not think my wife will make any difficulty about it. Will you also convey to my friends that I am very much obliged to them for the trouble they have taken and am quite satisfied with the result. I now see no reason why I should not be on friendly terms with my wife and children after a little, and see them from time to time. Of course I shall not make any attempt to see my children without my wife inviting me. I would not care to do so. It would be terrible to me if I thought I were to become a sort of bugbear to them and a source of terror to my wife. I am very pleased indeed that Mr Adrian Hope[1] is guardian. He is an old friend of mine, and a man of the highest character, as well as of intellectual and literary sympathies.

I would be much obliged to you if you would receive for

[1] A connection of Constance Wilde by marriage (1858–1904). He remained the official guardian of the children after Wilde and his wife were dead.

137

me this little income of £150, such as it is, as a prelude to your receiving for me any and all monies that may be in the future coming to me. I am quite incapable of managing my own affairs, and always have been. I don't know what to do with money except to throw it away. I would like to make all my arrangements for plays, books and the like, through you, and for you to receive all my earnings, small or big, so that I may know how I stand from time to time, and have your advice and help. I see no reason why I should not be making money in a year's time or so, and if one makes money at all by plays, one makes a good deal. My royalties for the *week* preceding my fatal and idiotic step of beginning an action at law were £245. Those were my halcyon days, which did me, I dare say, a lot of harm. I merely note it to show that there is money to be made by plays. In any case, with you to look after my money, I would know exactly how I stood, and how my affairs were going. I am most anxious never to have to appeal to my wife for money. I think it would be unfair to her. If you will kindly consent to my request, I will have my monies left with you, such as may be coming to me on my release, and I will try to live sensibly.

As regards my bankruptcy, there are, I believe, several small portmanteau full of my letters and papers at Humphreys'.[1] Also a small valise containing personal effects. I would like these to be removed from Humphreys' office and deposited somewhere else, where they would be safe. have suggested to Mr More Adey to try and get a small room in Hornton Street[2], where, for the present, my effects could be stored. I suppose I will have to write an order to Humphreys to surrender these things. Once they are secured, I could then, through you, have an application

[1] C.O. Humphreys (1828–1902): see p. 129.
[2] Where Adey lived in Kensington.

made for my discharge. At present, Humphreys having my things, I don't like to do so. He may come forward with another bill, or do something tedious. He has already had an enormous sum for my bankruptcy, but is insatiate for money.

Will you let my friend Mr More Adey know that Mr Frank Harris[1] has kindly offered to take me with him to Spain for a month on my release, paying all my expenses, and arranging everything beforehand. I propose, for many reasons, to accept this offer. It will do me a great deal of good. So my ideas about Brussels may stand over. After Mr Harris leaves me at San Sebastian, will you tell Mr Adey that I propose to make my way to the coast of France about Brest, near places like Morlaix or Quimper, in the Finisterre Department. I fancy that there I could find really bracing air, which is absolutely necessary to me after eighteen months in this relaxing Thames Valley, as well as freedom from English people. I have come to the conclusion that all the watering places on the Channel, from Calais to Dinan, would be impossible for me. But I don't think English people go to Finisterre or Morbihan. Will you ask Mr More Adey to get a *Murray's Guide*, and see what sort of places there are in the Finisterre district, and if the air is bracing. After Mr Frank Harris leaves me, I hope Mr Adey and Mr Ross will join me where I am, which will, I hope, be on the Brest coast. Mr Adey and Mr Ross will, I know, see how important for me in many ways this proposed expedition with Mr Frank Harris is. It is a most generous and kind, and indeed chivalrous offer, and I should like to know that my friends approve of my accepting it. I would then go directly from here to Mr Harris's house at Richmond, and see him there, and arrange my luggage etc. I would then meet Mr Harris abroad. He is anxious for us to start together, but for many reasons I think it would be better for me to meet him

[1] Author, editor and adventurer (1856–1931).

in France. I am very anxious that the journey should not be in the newspapers.

Perhaps you might send this letter to Mr Adey, who will then return it to you; this would save the trouble of copying.

I am much obliged to you, pray let me say again, for your kind interest in my unfortunate affairs. I am glad to hear that they are showing signs of some slight improvement. Yours                                                    OSCAR WILDE


## To A.D. Hansell[1]

*21 April 1897*                                    *H.M. Prison, Reading*

Dear Sir, I suppose you duly received my letter of the 12th inst accepting the terms finally agreed on with reference to my interest in my marriage settlement?

I write now to ask you whether the requisite deeds — I suppose one deed at any rate will be requisite? — will be ready before my release. There is, as you know, no doubt, a difficulty about signing deeds abroad, the difficulty of proper attestation and the like, and as I shall not live or travel under my own name I might find some difficulty in the case of an English Consulate, supposing the deed required attestation there. There is also the trouble of postal arrangements, and the invariable bother of getting registered letters if one has no passport. Under these circumstances I think it would be very convenient if everything could be settled before my release, and I would like to see you personally once again, if you would be so kind as to come in person. The deeds themselves will I suppose be drawn up by Mr Hargrove, and at my wife's expense. On an application to the Commissioners you can of course have an inter-

[1] From a copy in a clerkly hand in the Hyde collection.

view — in a private room and without the presence of an Officer.

I would be much obliged if you would let Mr More Adey know that I would very much like to see him and Mr Ross before my release, to arrange about my movements on the day of my leaving prison and my subsequent position abroad. They have most kindly promised to meet me, and look after me. I feel very nervous and agitated about the ordeal of returning to the world, from the mere point of view of my own mental and [word omitted] balance, and I am anxious to have everything arranged beforehand. If they could come on Saturday week the first of May, I think it would be a good occasion. They must of course apply to the Commissioners for an interview of one hour in the Solicitor's Room. The presence of a Warder is not any longer made troublesome or distressing, so they need not apply to have it private. I have received, would you kindly inform them, a letter from Mr Ricketts. He is greatly disappointed at not seeing me, as he is anxious to publish something by me as soon as possible, and for other reasons. So, if they do not mind I would like them to bring Mr Ricketts with them. He is, besides being a most distinguished artist, an old friend of mine, and seems hurt at my not having let him see me on the occasion of the last visit, when he made special application.[1] You might mention to Mr Adey, to whom perhaps you will send this letter for the sake of convenience, that I have no intention at present of accepting Mr Ricketts's kind offer to accompany me into a Trappist monastery on my release.

Would you also kindly ask Mr Adey and Mr Ross from me to send a list of novels for me as soon as possible. I will add some myself to their list as I find that the prison library

[1] Ricketts did join the others on the next visit, but his presence was not a success (see *Letters*, p. 541).

has hardly any novels of Walter Scott's, and none of Thackeray's. I merely want Mr Ross to note down any new ones by such new writers as Stanley Weyman, Wells and others: also any new ones by Stevenson, whose *Treasure Island*, which I presented to the prison library some six weeks ago, is, I am informed by the Schoolmaster, in great request and much appreciated.[1]

Should you be kind enough to come and see me, you would, of course, come between the 1st May and the 19th, the date of my release.

I am sending today a petition to the Home Secretary, by kind permission of the Governor, to ask him to let me leave prison a few days before the 19th, as I am anxious to avoid the annoyance of journalists, and interviews, and people who might come here to gratify curiosity or inflict annoyance. The [*word omitted*] and routine of officialism may interfere with my request, but I am not without hope that they will see that it would be on all sides more seemly for my release to take place quietly and without scene or public attention of any kind. I suppose I shall have an answer before I see Mr Adey.

I remain, with many thanks for your kindness, truly yours
OSCAR WILDE

The question of my application for my Release in Bankruptcy had better stand over till the 1st of May, as I believe that Mr Humphreys has not merely my papers but also a travelling bag containing clothes etc. I wish Mr Adey would find out what Mr Humphreys has[2].

---

[1] Stevenson had died in 1894, but *Vailima Letters* (1895), *Weir of Hermiston* (1896) and *Songs of Travel* (1896) had been published posthumously.

[2] The two words omitted from this letter may have proved illegible to the copyist.

# William Dixon[1] to Wilde

## MS. Clark

*8 May 1897    The Red House, Hadlow, Tonbridge, Kent*

Dear Sir, Please allow me to offer you my best wishes for success on gaining your freedom.[2] I am a stranger to you but my heart goes out to any human being who has been so tempted as to fall. I am only twenty-two years old but I have shared a fate similar to your own. I fell a victim to the love of money and in my endeavours to satisfy my selfish desires I forged my employer's signature. Certainly there were circumstances connected with the case which in some degree lightened the weight of my crime, but the fact remains that I fell. After wandering about for nearly two months I felt a desire to rid myself of so great a strain and this feeling led me to confess my guilt. I was not tried until last November and received the exceedingly light sentence of four months' hard labour. I went through this term with an anxious desire to conquer my weak point and I hope I may have succeeded. I was released on the 18th of last March and since then I have been doing the secretarial work connected with a Children's Country Holiday Home. I had to either come here or go to a Labour Home of the Church Army.

I am writing to ask if you will take compassion on me and have me to assist you in your future work. I feel that I could be of service to you; I write shorthand, can operate the typewriter, and have a taste for literary work which I think might develop into something better with utility. When I was eighteen months old I lost the use of my left arm through paralysis but this makes very little difference in my

---

This is the man who, Wilde suggested to Ross, might type the *De profundis* letter (*Letters*, p. 614), but the suggestion appears to have been abandoned (*Letters*, pp. 622, 624).

Wilde was released from prison on 19 May 1897.

143

work. I have no father; my mother is cook-housekeeper t
Mrs Ewart, sister-in-law to the Queen's Equerry. I do no
want any salary but if you would take me I should b
satisfied with being clothed and fed.

If you cannot see your way to comply with my reques
then no harm has been done. It is only a desire to have
friend who would take an interest in me, and a wish to b
of service to you that has induced me to write this strang
appeal. I will treat any correspondence in strict confidence

In any case you have my best wishes for your futur
welfare. Believe me, dear sir, yours faithfully

WILLIAM DIXO

# BERNEVAL

1897

## To Edward Rose[1]
MS. Private

[Postmark 29 May 1897]
*Hôtel de la Plage, Berneval-sur-Mer*

*Private*

Dear Edward Rose, Whenever my friends came to see me in prison they always told me of charming notes and recognitions of my work as a dramatist, in articles above your name[2] and I write now — my first opportunity since my release — to tell you what pleasure it gave me to know that amongst those who write on the aesthetic of the drama in England there was, at any rate, one who remembered my work, and desired to recall it to his own or public memory. The French were charming to me all the time, and produced my play *Salome*, and wrote about me as a living artist, but the English denied me even the barren recognition one gives to the dead.

I am sure you will be pleased to know that I hope to be able to write again, and that I feel that while there is much that I have lost, still there was much that was not worth keeping. I am more of an individualist in morals than before, but I see clearly that my life was one quite unworthy of an artist in its deliberate and studied materialism.

I am delighted to hear of your two great successes: your laurels are perhaps sere or sun-scorched to you now, but to me they are fresh and green, as I have only just heard of them: indeed to you also they should be fresh and green, as

[1] Dramatist, actor, dramatic critic, reformer (1849–1904). One of the founders of Letchworth Garden City. His dramatisations of Anthony Hope's *The Prisoner of Zenda* and Stanley Weyman's *Under the Red Robe* were both produced in London in 1896.
[2] In 1896 Rose wrote five times about Wilde in the *Sunday Times*, describing *Lady Windermere's Fan* as "that high-water mark of dramatic literature".

147

you won them in a difficult and dangerous contest: to adapt requires the most subtle tact of selection and reconstruction and I hear from my friends how quite admirable the art of your two adaptations was. I wish very much I could have seen your *Prisoner of Zenda*[1], but I was occupied perforce with my own tragedy, one terrible in its origin and result, but from which I may gain — perhaps have gained — something not without high import for my life and art.

France has given me a lovely asylum, and many charming notes of sympathy, and, I may almost say, welcome: she is the modern mother of all artists, and has many wilful sons whom she always consoles and sometimes heals. For the moment I have, to avoid the prying eye and the foolish tongue, taken a curious name — M. Sebastian Melmoth — so, should you care to send me a line ever to tell me of your work, pray address me by my new title. Perhaps it sounds stranger to you than it does even to me. *Melmoth* is the name of that curious novel of my grand-uncle — Maturin — which thrilled Goethe, and *les jeunes romantiques*, and to which Balzac wrote a fascinating epilogue years ago. The book is now an extinct volcano, but I come from it like Empedocles, I hope, if the gods prove kind to one who denied them.[2]

Pray keep — as you no doubt will — this name and my address a secret. I write to pay in words a debt I am proud to still owe you. Truly yours OSCAR WILDE

[1] It opened on 7 January 1896, at the St James's Theatre, with George Alexander in the double leading role. According to Shaw, he played the drunk scene "like a seasoned teetotaller".

[2] *Melmoth the Wanderer* by Charles Robert Maturin (1782–1824) was published in 1820. Empedocles was a Sicilian poet and philosopher (*c.* 493–*c.* 433 B.C.). According to one tradition, he ended his life by plunging into the boiling crater of Mount Etna in order to prove his divinity.

# To Edward Strangman[1]

MS. Hyde

*Tuesday, 15 June [1897]*                    *Berneval-sur-Mer*

My dear Edward Strangman, Thank you so much for the books — just what I wanted. Dieppe, like all provincial towns in France, not merely has no books, but does not know in what garden those yellow flowers grow. Thank you, still more, for your charming letter, and all the gracious and gentle things you say to me, and of me. I hope you will write to me from time to time: I should be sorry to think that we passed as ships in the night, for in my *livre d'or* — my little book where I write the names of my friends — your name is written.

I want you very much to know Lord Alfred Douglas. He is at 25 Boulevard des Capucines. Pray write to him and tell him you have seen me, and would like to see him. He is a most delicate and refined poet, and has a personality of singular charm. I have not seen him yet, but I am going to let him come and see me in a few days. Our lives are divided, but we love each other deeply and our souls touch in myriad ways through the estranging air.

I hope to see you again before the year burns out to ashes, and am always sincerely yours                    OSCAR WILDE

[1] Born 1866. Wilde described him to Douglas as "a very gentle, rather shy chap: Irish by race, Oxford by culture, a friend of Will Rothenstein and Robbie, and a good friend of mine". He was called to the Bar in 1898, but it is now apparent (see p. 174) that at this time he was employed in some capacity by Smithers. William Rothenstein (1872–1945) was an artist, knighted in 1931.

# To Edward Strangman
MS. Hyde

*20 July [1897]*        [*Chalet Bourgeat*] *Berneval-sur-Mer*

My dear Strangman, I was really afraid you had gone to learn strange tongues in some other planet, and was quite anxious. But when the delightful books and the mystical tobacco arrived I knew not merely that you were alive, but that you were thinking of me, and both things were delightful to me.

I wish so much you were here. I am in my chalet, and am beginning work, but I find I can only work about an hour and a half at a time: after that I am utterly prostrate. However I have nearly finished a poem,[1] which I hope the *Chronicle* — reckless in art — will publish. I like what I have done very much, though it is a new style for me. I am out-Henleying Kipling![2] — but you will get a copy, and judge.

As regards Mirbeau,[3] of course Réjane[4] is out of Paris, and you know how difficult a *comédienne* is to catch. Their disguises off the stage are bewildering.

This is only a line to thank you sincerely for your letter and the delightful books. The tobacco is to be smoked gravely in a pipe. Do write sometimes to me. Sincerely yours

OSCAR WILDE

---

[1] *The Ballad of Reading Gaol.*
[2] W.E. Henley, poet, journalist and editor (1849–1903). On 22 February 1890 in his *Scots Observer* he had published Kipling's poem "Danny Deever", which tells of the hanging of a soldier for shooting a sleeping comrade.
[3] Octave Mirbeau (1850–1917), French author and journalist. During the early part of Wilde's imprisonment Mirbeau defended him in the French press.
[4] Leading French actress (1856–1920).

## To Reginald Turner[1]

MS. Mason

*Tuesday* [*3 August 1897*]                    *Berneval-sur-Mer*

Dearest Reggie, I am so sorry you are ill: I was in hopes of seeing you here soon. Do get well, and come over. I long for your delightful companionship and sympathetic friendship. The horizon of the English stage seems dark with Hichens.[2] Do finish your play and stop him.

Robbie was to have come here yesterday, but has not arrived. I suspect a conspiracy with ramifications. I suppose ramifications are a sort of dagger?

I wrote to you care of Bosie to thank you for the lovely clock: I hope he forwarded my letter. The clock *still goes*: and is quite astounding in its beauty and industry. It even works at night, when no one is watching it.

Aubrey, and Conder,[3] and Dal Young[4] are at Dieppe, and the place is very full. I have made Aubrey buy a hat more silver than silver: he is quite wonderful in it.

Do get well soon. Ever yours affectionately      OSCAR

[1] Journalist, novelist and wit (1869–1938).
[2] Robert Hichens, novelist (1864–1950). His play *The Daughters of Babylon*, written with Wilson Barrett, was running at the Lyric Theatre. It was later published as a novel (1899). His first novel *The Green Carnation* (1894) contained amusing but dangerous skits on Wilde and Douglas.
[3] Aubrey Beardsley (1872–98) and Charles Conder (1868–1909), artists. Beardsley had illustrated the English edition of *Salome*.
[4] Dalhousie Young, composer and pianist (1866–1921).

# To Laurence Housman[1]
TS. Clark

9 August [1897]          Chalet Bourgeat, Berneval-sur-Mer

Dear Mr Housman, I cannot tell you how gratified and touched I was to receive your charming letter, and the beautiful book that it so gracefully heralded.

Your prose is full of cadence and colour, and has a rhythmic music of words that makes that constant appeal to the ear, which, to me, is the very condition of literature. The "King's Evil", the "Tree of Guile", and the "Heart of the Sea" are quite beautiful: and their mysticism, as well as their meaning, touches me very deeply: and while they are of course dramatic, still one is conscious — as one should be in all objective art – of one personality dominating their perfection all through.

The whole book, with its studied and imaginative decorations and its links of song, is a very lovely and almost unique work of art. Your title pleases me little, but every one has some secret reason for christening a child: some day you must tell me yours. Ricketts and Shannon,[2] those good kind friends of mine, are coming to see me this month. It would be charming if you came with them.

I have lately been reading your brother's lovely lyrical poems,[3] so you see you have both of you given me that rare thing happiness. With renewal of my thanks, believe me truly yours          OSCAR WILDE

---

[1] Poet, dramatist, novelist and artist (1865–1959). The book he sent Wilde was his *All-Fellows*, a book of imaginary legends (1896).

[2] Charles Hazlewood Shannon (1863–1937), artist and close friend of Ricketts, designed the bindings of Wilde's last four plays.

[3] *A Shropshire Lad* by A.E. Housman (1859–1936), published in 1896. A.E.H. wrote in 1928: "Robert Ross told me that when he visited his friend in jail he learnt some of the poems by heart and recited them to him."

## To Laurence Housman
TS. Clark

*22 August 1897*          *Chalet Bourgeat, Berneval-sur-Mer*

Dear Mr Housman, Thank you for your kind letter. I hope some day to see you here, or elsewhere.

It is absurd of Ricketts and Shannon not to see the light lyrical beauty of your brother's work, and its grace and delicate felicity of mood and music. I can understand Ricketts not liking them, for he is dominated by the sense of definite design and intellectual architecture, nor can he see the wonderful strangeness of simple things in art and life: but Shannon is inexcusable: you must get him alone, and read them to him: you can tell him I think your brother's poems exceedingly like his own lithographs!

With regard to what you ask me about myself — well, I am occupied in finishing a poem, terribly realistic for me, and drawn from actual experience, a sort of denial of my own philosophy of art in many ways. I hope it is good, but every night I hear cocks crowing in Berneval, so I am afraid I may have denied myself, and would weep bitterly, if I had not wept away all my tears. I will send it to you, if you allow me, when it appears. Believe me truly yours

OSCAR WILDE

## Thomas Martin[1] to Robert Ross
MS. Clark

*26 August 1897*          *Holborn Union Workhouse,*
*Shepherdess Walk, City Road, E.C.*

Dear Sir, I beg to acknowledge with thanks the receipt of

[1] Coming to Reading Gaol as a warder some seven weeks before Wilde's release, he constantly broke the regulations to bring him extra food, as well as the *Daily Chronicle* and other papers. He was dismissed from the prison service for giving a sweet biscuit to a tiny child prisoner.

153

your letter and also what was enclosed therein,[1] for which I am much obliged. I will return it to you on the 25th September as I specified in my letter to Mr Wilde. You must not think that any little service which I was able to render Mr Wilde was done with a view of receiving reward, for as a matter of fact I would not have accepted anything had circumstances turned out differently; indeed I mentioned as much to him prior to his departure. The six pounds which you have already forwarded I intend to repay at the earliest opportunity.

The only thing which I regret is that I did not do more for him. But he never would take anything which I could have carried in without creating suspicion. I often suggested Bovril, some spirits and even a cigar; however he wouldn't accept either. The risk attached to edibles is very great owing to the bulk, safe enough in winter when overcoats are worn. I am, sir, yours respectfully          T. MARTIN

---

[1] Money sent by Wilde (see *Letters*, p. 602).

# NAPLES

1897-98

## To Leonard Smithers[1]
MS. Colgate

*Thursday, 14 [October 1897]*        *Villa Giudice, Posilippo*

My dear Smithers, I have just sent you off another telegram, and I do really hope you will not treat it as you did the others.

As I wrote to you five days ago, I am not asking you for a private loan, but for an advance on the profits of my work,[2] and I again say that considering that I declined to take advantage of your quixotic and generous offer of all the profits, and that I also declined to let my work appear in any paper, so as to leave you a fair field, and by that of course gave up a sum much larger than a wretched £20, I say that, considering this, my claim for a small advance is perfectly just and right. For three weeks you have been writing to me that you will send this sum "in a few days": "It is a question of days simply" you say in your letter of a *fortnight* ago. It really is too absurd and annoying to be treated in this way. In old days, my dear Smithers, you would have treated me very differently. But you remind me now in a very practical manner of my loss of power and position. Sincerely yours
O.W.


## To Leonard Smithers
MS. Harrow

*Wednesday [27 October 1897]*        *Villa Giudice, Posilippo*
*[Postmark 28 October 1897]*

My dear Smithers, I send you to-day the manuscript[3] of my poem and enclose two more verses for insertion on page 10.

[1] Publisher (1861–1907), whom Wilde had met at Dieppe in July. He was to publish Wilde's last three books.
[2] *The Ballad of Reading Gaol.*
[3] The typewritten fair copy of *The Ballad of Reading Gaol* as corrected by Wilde. See *Letters*, p. 667.

I really think the poem is now as good as I can make it. So when the type is fixed pray have it set up.

I trust that the ridiculous Pinker[1] — so unworthy, it seems, of his name — has done something. I rest my hopes on the *New York Journal*. They have millions, and like what is calculated to make a stir of some kind, or any kind.[2]

"Sweet Catullus' all-but-island, olive-silvery Sirmio"[3] is in the Italian Lakes, so I cannot take flowers to the tomb of your poet just at present.[4]

You say in your last letter that you object to being "*Reynolds*-ized",[5] but I think you might have remembered that you were writing to a confirmed "Smithersist". The observation was quite unnecessary.

I saw the other day in the museum here the bust of a young man of grave, somewhat severe beauty, and the most delicate refinement of type, rather like a young Oxonian of a very charming kind, the expression a mixture of pride and *ennui*. On referring to the catalogue I found it was the Emperor *Heliogabalus*; it was most curious and has filled me with a desire to write his life. Of course I shall publish it with you. His marriage with the moon, just referred to in *Dorian Gray*, would make a beautiful chapter of coloured words.

I am beginning to feel very nervous about America. Per-

[1] James Brand Pinker (1863–1922), literary agent.
[2] This paper had been bought in 1895 by the notorious William Randolph Hearst (1863–1951) who favoured every form of sensationalism.
[3] The last line of Tennyson's "*Frater Ave atque Vale*", in which he adapts the first line of Catullus's poem in praise of Sirmio on Lake Garda, where he lived.
[4] In 1894 Smithers published an English version of the poems of Catullus in prose and verse, "the metrical part by Captain Sir Richard F. Burton . . . . and the prose portion, introduction, and notes by Leonard C. Smithers". Sir Richard Burton (1821–90), traveller and translator of *The Arabian Nights* (1885–88).
[5] *Reynolds News*, a popular and sensational Sunday newspaper, which Wilde had suggested for *The Ballad* (*Letters*, p. 663).

haps after all they won't have the poem, or if they do will not pay anything like my price. If *they* won't publish, you must publish simultaneously in New York: it might sell as a book there.

I am going to have a dedication. I don't put any initials or name. I simply say:

> When I came out of prison
> some met me with garments and with spices,
> and others with wise counsel.
> You met me with love.[1]

Please let me see it in some nice type. I think it a beautiful and simple dedication. I hope you do too. I hope to hear soon again from you. Sincerely yours          OSCAR WILDE


## To Leonard Smithers
MS. Lockwood[2]

*Saturday [Postmark 27 November 1897]*
*Villa Giudice, Posilippo*

Dear Smithers, Your good-natured disposition still *will* excite false hopes: it is its line of progress and perfection. I go to Cook's twice a day, but the fiver you said you hoped to send on Wednesday last does not flash through the wires.

As for the offer for my plays, I thought there might be a difference between advancing £20 on a poem, and purchasing for £50 two plays that have been great *successes*, have

---

[1] These words were addressed to Robbie Ross, but they did not appear in *The Ballad*.
[2] This letter appeared in *Letters* in an incomplete and inaccurate text, misdated by a year.

been admired etc, and belong to a series of published plays that were sold out almost at once.[1]

Your spending £1000 in paying debts seems to me awful. I cannot understand such extravagance. Where will you end if you go on like this? Bankruptcy is always in store for those who pay their debts. It is their punishment.

I hope proofs arrived safe, and that you will have decided on a *"format"* of importance. Also, *do* copyright in America: "Sixty millions of people, *all* fools!" to improve, or expand, Carlyle.[2] Ever yours                                                   o.

## To Leonard Smithers
TS. Clark[3]

*30 November [1897]*                                      *Villa Giudice*

My dear Smithers, Robbie Ross has just sent me a copy of a letter he has written you, in which he states that he finds he has no longer my confidence in business matters, and so does not wish to be connected with my affairs.[4] I write at once to

---

[1] There exists (MS. Bodley Head) a document signed by Wilde, which runs:

> Agreement made between Leonard Smithers and Oscar Wilde this 27th day of April 1899.
>
> Oscar Wilde agrees to sell to Leonard Smithers all his right and interest in the publication in book form of *An Ideal Husband* and *The Importance of Being Earnest* for thirty pounds and acknowledges the receipt of that sum.

[2] "Consider, in fact a body of Six-hundred and fifty-eight miscellaneous persons set to consult about 'business', with Twenty-seven millions, mostly fools, assiduously listening to them" (*Latter-Day Pamphlets*, No VI, "Parliaments", 1850).

[3] Since this letter appeared in truncated form in *Letters* I have been able to complete it from a typescript in Clark.

[4] On learning that Wilde was living with Douglas, Constance had stopped his allowance. To Wilde's anger Ross and Adey had agreed that she was within her legal rights. For Ross's letter to Smithers of 25 November, see *Letters*, p. 688.

assure you that Robbie writes under a complete misapprehension, due to a misinterpretation of a phrase or sentence used by someone else. Robbie has done everything for me in business that anyone on earth could do, and his own generosity and unwearying kindness are beyond any expression of praise on my part, though, I am glad to say, not beyond my powers of gratitude. Robbie may not wish to be worried any more by my business affairs — he has had endless worry for two years over them, but it would be fairer of him to say that it is too much worry to go on, than that he finds he has not my confidence. Such a statement is childish and, if taken seriously by you, would lead you to think that I was at once dense of judgment and coarsely ungrateful in nature. Sincerely yours          OSCAR WILDE

## To More Adey
MS. Hyde

*Wednesday [15 December 1897]*          *Villa Giudice*

My dear More, A thousand thanks for your kindness in telegraphing the money. I return you the cheque defaced.[1]

I am going to Taormina for a few days as the guest of a Russian I have met here. He is very cultivated, and of advanced years.

I fear there is a dreadful misunderstanding about what I wrote to Adrian Hope. I simply said that I considered that Bosie had quite as good a *social* position as any of my other friends — and I think I was right in saying so. I would say

[1] Adey's cheque for £100 (MS. Hyde) made out to Sebastian Melmoth and dated 9 December 1897. This was half the sum he had received from Douglas's mother, Lady Queensberry (see *Letters*, p. 696). Presumably Wilde had been unable to cash the cheque, and had asked Adey to wire the money instead.

that A.D. had just as good a social position as Arthur Clifton for instance. There may be scandals about a person, and yet a person may have a high social position. For years I was an instance in point.

I judge that there has been some misrepresentation by Arthur Clifton writing to me that you and Robbie are deeply wounded with me because I have *"accused* you *of immorality"*! Can one imagine anything so absurd? In defending Bosie I claimed that he had a good social position — that was all.

But, of course, I am sorry that I wrote to *you* as I did. But I was unnerved, and pressure was put upon me — and I wrote without care or kindness — of course you must forgive me. I am sure you have done so already.

Delightful papers from Hornton Street keep arriving here — they are most welcome — and the letters on the English Academy very interesting.[1] With love to Robbie, Ever yours                                                    OSCAR

---

[1] The weekly *Academy* had published a list of forty names for a suggested English Academy of Letters. Wilde was not included. For details see *Letters*, p. 692.

# PARIS

—◁▷—

1898-1900

# To R.B. Cunninghame Graham[1]
MS. Edinburgh

[c. 20 February 1898]
                    Hôtel de Nice, Rue des Beaux-Arts, Paris

My dear Cunninghame Graham, A thousand thanks for your charming letter, and its generous, and most welcome, praise of *The Ballad*.

I read with great interest your article in the *Saturday* last June, and wish we could meet to talk over the many prisons of life — prisons of stone, prisons of passion, prisons of intellect, prisons of morality, and the rest. All limitations, external or internal, are prison-walls, and life is a limitation.

I hope you will be in Paris this spring, and come and see me. I often hear scraps of news about you from that good little chap Will Rothenstein. Ever yours    OSCAR WILDE


# To More Adey[2]

*Monday* [*21 February 1898*]                    *Hôtel de Nice*

My dear More, I see your beautiful handwriting on the cover of the *Echo*, which reached me this morning. Many sincere thanks. It is a capital review,[3] but, of course, I want the literary papers to criticise it. It is not *altogether* a

---

[1] The most picturesque Scot of his time, traveller, horseman, writer and Socialist campaigner (1852–1936). He had been imprisoned for his part in "Bloody Sunday" (see p. 108), and had described his prison experiences in "Sursum Corda", published in the *Saturday Review* on 19 June 1897, and reprinted in his book *Success* (1902).
[2] Text from a copy in the hand of Stuart Mason in the Clark collection.
[3] Of *The Ballad of Reading Gaol*, which had been published on 13 February. The *Echo* review appeared on 19 February.

pamphlet on prison-reform. I wonder what that good kind fellow Major Nelson[1] thinks of it. I sent him a copy.

I wish you could come over here and see me, but I suppose that is difficult. The intellectual atmosphere of Paris has done me good, and I now have ideas, not merely passions. Naples was fatal.

Are you writing?

Are you in love?

Are you happy? Ever yours                                                    O.W.

## To Rowland Strong[2]
TS. Clark

*Tuesday* [*February–March 1898*]                                 *Hôtel de Nice*

I send you a copy of my *Ballad*, which I hope you will accept with the author's compliments . . . . The copy is of the first edition, which, I am glad to say, has now some interest for the bibliophile, and fetches a high price in London: it was exhausted on the day of issue. The poem has been a great success, I am glad to say, and the Press has not boycotted it after all.                                        OSCAR WILDE

## To Rowland Strong
TS. Clark

[*February–March 1898*]                                           *Hôtel de Nice*

I cannot tell you what pleasure your letter gave me, I wish my poem had fallen into your hands for review. Though I have had some most sympathetic and intellectual criticisms,

[1] The benevolent Governor of Reading Gaol.
[2] 1865–1924. Paris correspondent of English and American papers. Much involved in the Dreyfus Case.

nothing that has been said about *The Ballad* has touched me, or encouraged me, as much as your letter . . . . In the meanwhile, have you any money to spare? If you have it would be very kind of you if you would lend me fifty francs. I am quite *sans le sou*, and awaiting money from my absurd publisher . . .                                        OSCAR WILDE

## To Laurence Housman
TS. Clark

[*February–March 1898*]                                 *Hôtel de Nice*

Dear Mr Housman, I am so glad you got the copy I ordered to be sent to you. I was in Naples, so had to deny myself the pleasure of writing your name on the fly-leaf.

I thank you very much for all you have said to me about *The Ballad*: it has greatly touched me. I quite hold with you on all you say about the relation of human suffering to art; as art is the most intense mode of expression, so suffering is the most real mode of life, the one for which we are all ultimately created.

I read some wonderful extracts from *Spikenard*[1] in the *Chronicle*, but to have the book itself would be a great honour and a great pleasure. Yours most sincerely       O.W.

## To Leonard Smithers
TS. Clark

*Tuesday* [? *1 March 1898*]                          *Hôtel de Nice*

Dear Smithers, Has the *Sketch* had a copy? If not, please send them one. Also, will you kindly send me a copy of the last edition in *sheets* — unsewn and unbound — so that I

[1] A book of poems by Laurence Housman published in 1898.

167

can give them to the printer of the *Mercure de France*. This pray do at once, as they go to press on the *fifteenth*.

The weather in Paris is quite awful — real snow and other horrors.

I wish you would look at the *Chansons de Bilitis* by Pierre Louÿs.[1] I think you could do something with it, privately of course, that is a very limited edition. Ernest[2] could translate it for you.

Will Rothenstein has written me a wonderful appreciation of *The Ballad* — really masterly.

Maurice[3] is quite well. I am now two games behind. I wish you could make him your agent here at a salary of £400 a year. My future would be (under Providence) assured. Ever yours                                              OSCAR

## To Leonard Smithers
MS. Lockwood[4]

*Thursday* [*Postmark 3 March 1898*]          [*Hôtel de Nice*]

My dear Smithers, Very well: no dedication for the Author's Edition.[5] You are always wise and prudent (about other people's affairs). Please send the money you promise for tomorrow in a bank-note, as no banks are open on Sunday.

---

[1] A volume of prose-poems (1894) by the French poet and novelist (1870–1925).
[2] Ernest Dowson, poet and translator (1867–1900).
[3] Maurice Gilbert, one of Wilde's closest and most devoted friends during these last years. They played innumerable games of bezique together.
[4] This letter appeared in *Letters* in an incomplete and inaccurate form.
[5] The third edition (March 1898), which consisted of ninety-nine numbered copies, signed by the author. It was published at ten shillings and sixpence, the other editions at two shillings and sixpence (or one guinea on Japanese vellum).

and I may not get it till too late on Saturday. I enclose an absurd review from the *Herald* — of today.

I think the poem will appear in a French edition, with translation, either in a book or a review.[1] This will be capital. I am not at all well, and also am very unhappy, but dear Robbie Ross is bestirring himself in my interests, like the good chap he is.

There is going to be a recitation in a French translation of some of my poems in prose at the Odéon — at a literary matinée.

Maurice has won twenty-five games of bezique and I twenty-four: however, as he has youth, and I have only genius, it is only natural that he should beat me. Ever yours

OSCAR WILDE

## To Leonard Smithers
MS. Lockwood[2]

*Postmark 4 March 1898*]                                    *Hôtel de Nice*

My dear Smithers, If we could have an edition at Boston or New York of even three hundred copies, I think that would be a start. I know you will work your best for it. Please send me the *Academy*. I have not seen it. Please do this at once, and also send me the *Saturday*, if A.S. has his article in it.[3]

I rely on your sending me a little money tomorrow. I have only succeeded in getting twenty francs from the concierge, and I am in a bad way. Do you really think that 10/- is enough for the Author's Edition? I should have thought

[1] The French translation by Henry D. Davray appeared in the May 1898 issue of the *Mercure de France*, and in book form in the autumn.
[2] This letter appeared in *Letters* in an incomplete and inaccurate form.
[3] Arthur Symons, whose review of *The Ballad* appeared in the *Saturday Review* on 12 March.

15/- was the least. Could you find out *who* wrote the
*Sunday Special*[1] notice? I want particularly to know, a:
Callan[2] says he did, and I feel curious. The *Athenaeun*
advertisement is splendid.[3]

Maurice and I are exactly quits now — twenty-six game.
each — but I have unfortunately lost my heart, which
carefully staked on a separate game. Ever yours      OSCAF

## To Leonard Smithers[4]

[*Postmark 20 March 1898*]                    *Hôtel de Nice*

My dear Smithers, I quite understand how you feel about
poor Aubrey.[5] Still, you, and you alone, recreated his art for
him, gave him a new and greater position, and for such
generous and enthusiastic service to art and to an artist you
will have your reward in Heaven: at least you will never
have it in this world.

I have not yet seen Vallette.[6] I simply wanted to know
the cost of an edition with a French translation — by you
and the Chiswick Press — as the type is set up. Can you give
me an idea — an edition of 500 copies? Also, do you not

[1] A Sunday newspaper which ran from December 1897 till December
1903. On 13 February 1898 (publication day) it had published the first
and most enthusiastic review of *The Ballad*, the anonymous reviewer
claiming that "not since the first publication of 'The Ancient Mariner'
have the English public been proffered such a weird, enthralling and
masterly ballad-narration."
[2] A young writer of whom Wilde wrote: "His style is somewhat colour-
less but he has purple hair."
[3] A large advertisement in the issue of 5 March, announcing the fourth
edition of *The Ballad*.
[4] Text from facsimile in *Oscar Wilde* by Philippe Jullian (1969). The
text in *Letters* is truncated and incorrect.
[5] Aubrey Beardsley, who had died on 16 March 1898, aged twenty-five.
Smithers had published much of his work.
[6] Alfred Vallette (1858–1935), founder and editor of the *Mercure de
France*.

hink that, if the cost be not too great, we might "*stereo-ype*"?

Have Smith's bookstalls taken the poem? If not, do work t — and supply them with a placard.

Could you have a leaflet, with criticisms, put into the eaves of a good magazine? like Pears' soap, and other more seful things. I think it would be profitable; in any case it would irritate the reader. The *Athenaeum* advertisement is admirable;[1] I feel like Lipton's tea. Ever yours          O.W.

## To Robert Ross
MS. Rosenbach

*Tuesday* [*? late April 1898*][2]

Dearest Bobbie, The idea for *The Ballad* came to me while I was in the dock, waiting for my sentence to be pronounced. Bosie must not say that he originated it.

I am very miserable. Ever yours          OSCAR

## To Leonard Smithers
MS. Clark

*Tuesday evening* [*10 May. Postmark 11 May 1898*] [*Paris*]

My dear Smithers, I have been *seven* times to Cook's, and also went at seven o'clock, two hours after their bank closes, and woke them up. Of course nothing at all had arrived, so I have had no dinner. I hope you had a good one. Ever yours
          O.W.

[1] It appeared on 19 March and was headed "3000 copies sold in three weeks."
[2] It is impossible to date this letter with certainty, but from its brevity it was probably written when Ross was in Paris. Constance Wilde died in Genoa on 7 April. Ross crossed to Paris to comfort Wilde, and was still there on 17 April. Douglas arrived in Paris towards the end of the month.

## To Edward Strangman
MS. Hyde

[*4 June 1898. Postmark 5 June*]

*Hôtel d'Alsace, Rue des Beaux-Arts, Par*

My dear Strangman, It will give me great pleasure to din
with you tomorrow (*Sunday*), and I will call for you at you
hotel at 7.45.

I do not know if you have wrecked the tables at Mont
Carlo, or returned with empty scrip, but if you have an
money to spare it would be very good of you if you coul
lend me even a hundred francs. I have been in a position a
once tragic and comic for some time, without money, an
with that detestable preoccupation with money that povert
entails — a mood of mind fatal to all fine things. I owe m
wretched hotel £14 for two months' lodging, and canno
either leave it or remain in it. Somehow my life has falle
on bitter ways.

However, to see you again will be a real pleasure, and
know we shall have a delightful evening. I have still a sui
of dress-clothes and to wear them will be an era! Mos
sincerely yours OSCAR WILD

## To Georgette Leblanc[1]

[*Early June 1898*] [*Paris*

Madame, I do not know how to thank you for the grea
pleasure you gave me last night at the theatre, and I beg you

[1] Actress and singer, mistress of the Flemish poet Maurice Maeterlinck
She had recently taken over from Emma Calvé the leading rôle i
Massenet's opera *Sapho* at the Opéra Comique.
    Text from *Maeterlinck and I* by Georgette Leblanc (1932). This is i
the main a translation from the French (by Janet Flanner) of G.L'
*Souvenirs* (1931), but the Wilde letter does not appear in the Frencl
edition.

o give me the honour of seeing you for five minutes. I should like to kiss the white and beautiful hands of one of the greatest and most distinguished artists I have ever seen.

Pleasure comes rarely to my life now; but last night I was happy. Beauty and genius can console. I offer you my homage and my thanks.                                    OSCAR WILDE


## To Leonard Smithers
MS. Koch

[23 November 1898][1]                                    *Grand Café*
                                    *14 Boulevard des Capucines, Paris*

My dear Smithers, I return second batch of proofs:[2] they are very good indeed. Send the third instalment as soon as possible.

I am writing to Shannon, but the binding will surely take some time? However, if Shannon does the three little designs, they will not take long to cut. In fact I think there is only one gilt petal repeated.[3]

Write to Alexander and ask him to let you have the *play-bill*, as that must be published, after the dedication. The title-page I suppose had better have "By the author of *Lady Windermere's Fan*".

Paris is dreadfully cold. Quite winter. I miss you very much. Much excitement has been caused by our supper, and I have now the reputation of being a "mulierast", as Robbie phrases it: it is very painful.

Kind regards to Strangman. Ever yours  OSCAR WILDE


[1] So dated in another hand.
[2] Of *The Importance of Being Earnest*.
[3] There was.

173

# To an Unidentified Correspondent[1]
## MS. Mason

*Saturday 26 November* [*1898*]            *Taverne F. Pousse*
                                    *14 Boulevard des Italiens, Pari*

My dear Frank, Thank you very much for your kind letter
My publisher brought over my clothes for me, so I won'
have to trouble you. I am delighted you are coming back
On £25 a month you should be able to manage, and whe
you are living abroad surely your people will come to terms

   The great thing is for you to learn French, which you
could do in six weeks, or two months. Every artist shoul
know French, and every gentleman.

   I suppose you will come first to the Hôtel d'Alsace. Afte
that you might look for rooms, so as to be close to th
Boulevards. I would be charmed to help you to get them. I
Harold coming? You give me no news of him.

   Paris is very purple, and starred with gilt spangles. Eve
yours                                              OSCA

# To Edward Strangman
## MS. Hyde

[*Postmark November 1898*]            *Hôtel d'Alsac*

My dear Strangman, I was so sorry not to see you when yo
last came to France. I now write to you, as, I believe, th
responsible partner of Smithers' firm, to ask you if yo
would advance me, on the part of the firm, £10 or £15 o
account of my play which you are publishing.

   I am in serious straits, and it would help me very much
If you can do this, would you let me have the money b
Saturday morning, as I am in trouble with my hotel. Eve
yours                                        OSCAR WILD

[1] Certainly *not* Frank Harris, as someone has suggested on the original

## To Leonard Smithers

MS. Texas

[*Postmark 1 December 1898*]        *Taverne F. Pousset*

My dear Smithers, I return the proofs. Will you kindly see if *Chasuble* is called "Chasuble" or "Doctor Chasuble" in Act II? If he is called "Doctor Chasuble" of course the title, in the headline, should be continued. Shannon will do the cover.

If you don't hear from Alexander, kindly ask one of your clerks to look up the *Era* for February 1895 — about the 14th — all the cast will be there. The *Era* newspaper, of course: also the *date* of the production must be given.

Shannon will send you the design in a few days. Of course you will have the same lovely cloth.

The original title was

> *The Importance of being Earnest:*
> *A Trivial Comedy for Serious People.*

Would this be too much for the title-page? I think not. You must add "by the author of *Lady Windermere's Fan*".

Paris is quite wintry: I have not returned to the Moulin Rouge. I hear Miss D'Or has no grandson. Ever yours  o.w.


## To Leonard Smithers

TS. Clark

[*c. 28 December 1898*]        *Hôtel des Bains, Napoule*

My dear Smithers, Do give me some news about my book, when it is to appear, etc.

I wish you would send me a *Volpone*, if you can spare one.[1] I am astounded not to have received a copy, and so is

---

[1] An edition of Ben Jonson's play, illustrated by Beardsley, with a eulogy of Beardsley by Robbie Ross, published by Smithers in a limited edition of a thousand copies.

Robbie Ross. I want to see how he writes eulogies. If they are as good as his lectures they should be admirable, but indeed everything that Robbie writes is admirable. I am always rebuking him for his idleness, which I attribute entirely to his early hours.

*Chronicles* arrive fitfully, usually in packets of two. Last week Monday's and Tuesday's were I suppose lost in the Channel storm: they have not appeared yet. And as the *Chronicle* has the absurd habit of not inventing its news, I suppose I have practically read them.

You will send me some ordinary title-pages for presentation copies. Also pray tell me how many I am to have of each edition.

I am leading a very good life, and it does not agree with me. There is a sad lack of fauns in the pinewoods at Napoule, and if the sea has its Proteus, he is always disguised as an elderly Member of Parliament. How is Pollitt?[1] He has sent me two photographs of himself: in one he is fair, in the other dark; and neither resembles the other. What is he like? Ever yours                                OSCAR

## To Laurence Housman
### TS. Clark

[*c. 28 December 1898*]                *Hôtel des Bains, Napoule*

My dear Housman, After your letter declaring the impossibility of coming here, I am surprised not to find you in the adjacent pinewoods, for these woods change the air to an aromatic: the wind that makes their branches restless is

---

[1] Herbert Charles Pollitt (1871–1942), a young man who had corresponded with Wilde. He collected Beardsley drawings, which he bought from Smithers.

pungent with keen odours: when one walks in their dappled shadows one's feet crush sweetness out of the fallen needles: and the still sweeter sun is as warm as wine, and coloured like an apricot.

I think your drawing lovely, so delicate in modulation of curve and line. I am sure Donatello would have liked it, and I wish I had ever written anything that Donatello would have liked.

The people here — fisher-folk all — have beautiful eyes, crisp hair of a hyacinth colour, and no morals: an ideal race. I have two special friends, one called Raphael, the other Fortuné — both quite perfect, except that they can read and write.

How wrong of the young Greek Alexander to be ill: it is mixing up two distinct and separate styles. I think a little want of sympathy would make him well: it has a wonderful effect on invalids. Send him, however, all nice phrases from me. Sincerely yours                    OSCAR WILDE


## To Leonard Smithers
TS. Clark

*13 January 1899*                    *Hôtel des Bains, Napoule*

My dear Smithers, Thanks so much for *Volpone*: it is a very fine issue indeed. I don't of course think Aubrey's designs at all up to his former work: nothing to *Salome* or *The Rape of the Lock*, or many other of his things, but the frontispiece is fascinating, and had he lived he would no doubt have done wonderful other illustrations. The cover I don't like. It would be a good one on rich texture, but it is not a good cover for a book. Bobbie's eulogy I think quite charming, and the preface is excellently written. The play is, I suppose, by you.

Certainly: twenty ordinary, five large-paper, and one

177

vellum for me — of my play. I hope to get the title-pages soon.[1]

Yes: even at Napoule there is romance: it comes in boats and takes the form of fisher-lads, who draw great nets, and are bare-limbed: they are strangely perfect. I was at Nice lately: romance there is a profession plied beneath the moon.

The *Chronicle now* arrives daily. Many thanks. Ever yours                                    OSCAR WILDE

## *To Leonard Smithers*[2]

[*c.* 1 *February* 1899]                *Hôtel des Bains, Napoule*

My dear Smithers . . . I have marked three Japanese-paper copies, as Strangman should have one; the two others are for you and Robbie. I enclose the names of the people I am sending to. Robbie can give you the addresses where I have forgotten them.

One large-paper has a smudge of ink on it, but as I have initialled the smudge, which I made myself, it must count as a *remarque.*[3] You might ask one and sixpence extra for that copy . . . I suppose the book will be out this month. I am probably changing my address, so don't send my copy till I write. Ever yours                                    O.W

---

[1] Of *The Importance of Being Earnest.* The ordinary edition was priced at seven shillings and sixpence, and the one hundred large-paper copies at one guinea. The twelve copies on Japanese vellum were for presentation only. The numbers and prices of *An Ideal Husband* were the same.

[2] Text from the Prescott sale catalogue of Christie's (New York) where, on 6 February 1981, this letter and the copy of the book with the initialled smudge together fetched $8500.

[3] i.e. an annotation.

178

## To Leonard Smithers
TS. Clark

*Saturday* [*18 February 1899*]    *Grand Café Glacier, Nice*

My dear Smithers, Why no answer to my telegram? It was sent last Wednesday. You are quite under a mistake in imagining that Frank Harris pays for me here. I wish he did. He has given me a little money on two occasions, but he does not pay for me, and he is very hard up. He is the only epicure who thoroughly appreciates his hotel, so l fear he is losing money.

Do send me at once £15, or £10 at any rate, by *wire*, *through Cook's* here, as I am stuck at my hotel and do not go to Switzerland till the 1st March. I must live till then. After March 1st I am all right for three months. *Pray do this* for me.

Also, let me have a copy of the book.[1] Send one to George Alexander with the compliments of the author and the publisher. And I forgot Arthur Clifton. Will you send him a copy from me. Robbie will give you his address, with enclosed slip. Ever yours                              OSCAR

## To Leonard Smithers
MS. Dalhousie[2]

*Saturday* [*24 February 1899. Postmark 25 February 1899*]
                                                            *Nice*

My dear Smithers, I leave tomorrow for Geneva. My address will be

---

[1] *The Importance of Being Earnest*, which was published in February.
[2] An incomplete version of this letter appeared in *Letters*, p. 782.

M. Sebastian Melmoth
c/o Harold Mellor[1]
Gland
Canton Vaud
La Suisse

Please send the £30 there — also a copy of the play. I have not yet seen it. I hope the large-paper are finished by this. Have my other copies been sent out? I have received no acknowledgment from anyone. Ever yours          O.W.


## To Leonard Smithers
MS. Lockwood[2]

[*Postmark 18 March 1899*]                                    *Gland*

My dear Smithers, I am sending you off the manuscript.[3] I think it reads very well now. Corrections are a great trouble — worse than a new play. I am quite exhausted.

Rose's address is surely *St James's Theatre*. Shaw's copy should go to his publisher's care. Do have them sent off at once.

No money from you! This is dreadful. Do let me have £5 *at once*. Mellor carries out the traditions of the ancient misers. If I ask him to lend me five francs he grows yellow and takes to his bed. Every day I discover some new fault in him. The way he grows on one is awful — and he gives me Swiss wine to drink!

I look on you as owing me £25, so really £5 by return is nothing, but do send it *at once*. Ever yours          O.W.

---

[1] A wealthy and neurotic recluse (1868–1925), whom Wilde had met in the South of France.
[2] This letter appeared in truncated and inaccurate form in *Letters*.
[3] Of *An Ideal Husband*. It was four years since this play and *The Importance of Being Earnest* had been performed. Wilde had no rehearsal copies, and was forced to try and remember the alterations and improvements that had been made in rehearsal.

## To Leonard Smithers

TS. Clark

*Saturday* [*25 March 1899*]                    *Gland, Switzerland*

My dear Smithers, Thanks very much for the fiver, duly received. Of course the stage directions are to be in italics.[1]

As regards the other, the words in the spoken text, I am not very fond of spacing, but I am not at all fond of italics for *single* words. Let us try spacing, for a beginning. Indeed I am ready to leave the thing in your hands.

Acts 3 and 4 have arrived, beautifully typewritten. I will send them on Tuesday. I really think it reads the best of my plays.

Were *all* my presentation copies sent off?[2] Most of them have been treated with silent horror or indifference. I must advertise for some new friends. I don't want any certificates of good character. I should in fact object to them. Perhaps you could help me in the matter.

Mellor is still tedious and unbearable. I simply cannot stand him. I wish I could get away.

Have you got the playbill, with date? Have you settled with Shannon? There are no cocottes at Gland for you. There is one, I hear, at Geneva, but one has to send in applications for shares at least six weeks in advance. I hope Dowson got his copy? Robbie seems very depressed, and rather Canadian. Have you been giving him manuscripts to read? How is Strangman? Did *he* get his copy? His silence on the subject is deafening. Ever yours                    OSCAR

---

[1] Of *An Ideal Husband*, which Smithers published in July 1899.
[2] Of *The Importance of Being Earnest*.

## To Kyrle Bellew[1]

MS. Hyde

[*Postmark 7 May 1899*]

*Hôtel de la Néva, Rue Montigny, Paris*

My dear Kyrle, I have waited to answer your letter till my arrival in Paris, where I can be in closer communication with London.

It would give me great pleasure to work with you on any play: will you let me know what the play is: is it an original play? Is it modern as regards time, place, and treatment? Could you send it to me? Is there any chance of your being able to come over here with it? The latter course would be the better.

It was delightful hearing from you again, and I thank you very much for the continuance of our old friendship: to see you here for a couple of days would be charming.

Pray give my kindest regards to Mrs Brown Potter, of whose brilliant successes, as of yours, I hear on all sides, and believe me sincerely yours                OSCAR WILDE


## To Ada Rehan[2]

MS. Clark

[*8 June 1899*]                                                    [*Paris*]

My dear Miss Rehan, I need not say how shocked and distressed I was to read in the papers this morning of the terrible tragedy that has occurred.

---

[1] English actor (1855–1911). He had long been associated with the actress Cora Brown Potter (1859–1936).
[2] American actress (1860–1916) who had achieved considerable success in New York and London, always under the management and direction of Augustin Daly, who died in Paris on 7 June 1899. Wilde had met them both a few days earlier (see *Letters*, p. 800).

His death is a great loss to art: an irreparable loss to the American stage: his cultivation, his unerring instinct, his love and knowledge of literature, his high sense of the drama as a form of art — all gave him a unique position: and all artists mourn him, for all artists appreciated him.

What his loss is to you I hardly dare to think: his life-long devotion to your genius is known to us all: and in you he found someone whose brilliancy of imagination, whose magic of personality, whose mastery over every mode of dramatic art, could help him to realise and give form to all he dreamed of. It was a noble comradeship — and if Death has, for the moment, broken it, it was because only Death could do so.

Pray, dear and wonderful lady, let me again tell you of the deep sympathy all feel for you. Your own sorrow has echoes everywhere. His name will by others also be held in affectionate remembrance. For yourself, in art alone is there consolation for the artist. None knows that better than I. Your sincere friend and admirer OSCAR WILDE

## To Robert Ross
MS. Prague

[*July 1899*]     *L' Île d' Amour, Chennevières-sur-Marne*

My dear Robbie, Smithers has sent me the August allowance, so don't send me anything.

This is a line to beg you to come here: a lovely spot — an island, with trees and a little inn. 6.50 francs a day, *tout compris*. Do come. Ever yours OSCAR

## To Arthur L. Humphreys
MS. Maguire

*Sunday [August 1899]*                                     *Hôtel d'Alsace*

My dear Humphreys, I am so glad you received your copy of
my play all right. I think it looks very nice in its pale purple
and noble gold. I hope it will do well, but I don't think the
reviewers have written anything yet. It is very horrid of
them, and very stupid.

I was greatly delighted, I need hardly tell you, with what
you wrote about my work in your monthly message,[1] and the
footnote was admirable. If the critics had your sense of literature and of life they would treat me in a different manner.

Paris is burning hot — streets of brass in which the
passers — few in number — crawl like black flies. I wish I
had the means to go away, but I am in dreadful want — no
money at all. I wonder would you lend me £5? If you could
I think you would. I have been passing through a terrible
time. Sincerely yours                                     OSCAR WILDE

## To Robert Ross
MS. Private

*[Late February 1900]*                                     *Hôtel d'Alsace*

My dear Robbie, Will you, like a good fellow, send me a
cheque for my two months, £27.10. is it not?

I don't write, *nor do you*, I don't know why.

I am now *neurasthenic*. My doctor says I have all the
symptoms. It is comforting to have them *all*, it makes one
a perfect type.

Paris is awful. I have also been poisoned by mussels — a
dreadful thing.

I hope to write soon. Ever yours                                     OSCAR

[1] Presumably to Hatchard's customers.

184

## To Frank Harris
### MS. Hyde

*[? June] 1900*　　　　*Grand Café, 14 Boulevard des Capucines,*
*Paris*

My dear Frank, I think you had better come over at once.
I suppose it is all right, but you seem to me to be very
"previous". I met an American journalist yesterday who
knew all about your interviews with Mrs Brown Potter —
was present, I believe. I want to know what is going on —
that is all. So come over. Ever yours　　　　OSCAR


## Frank Harris to Wilde
### MS. Clark

*26 September 1900*　　　　*Élysée Palace Hôtel, Paris*

Dear Oscar, I have already put aside for you five hundred
(500) Ordinary Shares in the Cesari Reserve Syndicate and
I now declare that I owe you these and shall deliver the
certificate to you within a week. Yours sincerely

FRANK HARRIS[1]


## To Frank Harris
### MS. Hyde

*[Postmark 22 October 1900]*　　　　*Hôtel d'Alsace*

My dear Frank, I must ask you to carry out your agreement.
Three weeks ago you engaged to pay me £175 within a week.
I trusted you so completely that I actually gave you a receipt

---

[1] Harris had many faults, but lack of generosity to Wilde was not one of
them. No doubt these shares were worthless, but they were clearly well
meant.

185

for the *entire sum*, although £25 was all you gave me. Fully believing in you I arranged to be operated on by one of the first surgeons in Paris: the operation took place ten days ago under chloroform. I was obliged to draw post-dated cheques for the fees, which were enormous. I have also been obliged to have a *garde-malade* by day, and a doctor to sleep in the same room at night, besides a consulting physician. My debts and expenses are appalling — not less than £150. I relied on your honour to carry out your agreement.

You assured me that I had a perfect legal right to sell you my plot,[1] that you had taken legal advice on the matter etc. Now you calmly tell me that you propose to give Kyrle Bellew £125 of my money.

I cannot let you do so: I do not allow you to do so: you have no right to pay to anyone the money you owe me, and I must insist on your sending me £125 now owing to me for nearly two weeks. It is outrageous your leaving me as I am, ill, in bed, operated on twice a day, in continuous pain, and without a penny. You owe me this money. It was merely to be able to pay for this operation that I consented to this absurd agreement between us. I wanted money to save my life, which was at stake. You induce me to trust you, I sign away my play, and you send me a paltry £25. My surgeon's fee is £50, my consulting physician £35, and my other expenses not less than £60 — and you calmly let me go to utter ruin, having got the agreement out of me.

You told me I had a legal right to sell my plot: you engaged to pay me more, which you never have paid. You prepared the agreement, and left *me* to your word of honour. Well, I have your agreement and your word of honour, and I ask you to send me by return £125 that you owe me. Ever yours                                   OSCAR

[1] Of the play that Harris later wrote as *Mr and Mrs Daventry*. For Wilde's original scenario, and a list of the people to whom he sold the rights, see *Letters*, pp. 360–62 and 829.

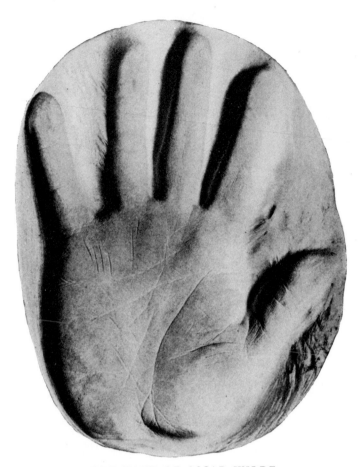

THE HAND OF OSCAR WILDE

Photographed by the fortune-teller Mrs Robinson, whom Wilde consulted in 1894 (see *Letters*, p. 358), and called the Sybyl of Mortimer Street. She told him "I see a very brilliant life for you up to a certain point. Then I see a wall. Beyond the wall I see nothing." She reproduced the photograph, without Wilde's name, in her book *The Graven Palm* (1911). For Wilde's continued interest in palmistry see his short story *Lord Arthur Savile's Crime* (1887) and page 199 of this book.

---

# MR OSCAR WILDE ON MR OSCAR WILDE

*An Interview*[1]

I found Mr Oscar Wilde (writes a Representative) making ready to depart on a short visit to Algiers, and reading, of course, nothing so obvious as a time-table, but a French newspaper which contained an account of the first night of *An Ideal Husband* and its author's appearance after the play.

"How well the French appreciate these brilliant wilful moments in an artist's life," remarked Mr Wilde, handing me the article as if he considered the interview already at an end.

"Does it give you any pleasure," I inquired, "to appear before the curtain after the production of your plays?"

"None whatsoever. No artist finds any interest in seeing the public. The public is very much interested in seeing an artist. Personally, I prefer the French custom, according to which the name of the dramatist is announced to the public by the oldest actor in the piece."

"Would you advocate," I asked, "this custom in England?"

"Certainly. The more the public is interested in artists, the less it is interested in art. The personality of the artist is not a thing the public should know anything about. It is too accidental." Then, after a pause —

"It might be more interesting if the name of the author were announced by the *youngest* actor present."

"It is only in deference, then, to the imperious mandate

---

[1] Published in the *St James's Gazette*, 18 January 1895. For its probable authorship see p. 128.

of the public that you have appeared before the curtain?"

"Yes; I have always been very good-natured about that. The public has always been so appreciative of my work I felt it would be a pity to spoil its evening."

"I notice some people have found fault with the character of your speeches."

"Yes, the old-fashioned idea was that the dramatist should appear and merely thank his kind friends for their patronage and presence. I am glad to say I have altered all that. The artist cannot be degraded into the servant of the public. While I have always recognized the cultured appreciation that actors and audience have shown for my work, I have equally recognized that humility is for the hypocrite, modesty for the incompetent. Assertion is at once the duty and privilege of the artist."

"To what do you attribute, Mr Wilde, the fact that so few men of letters besides yourself have written plays for public presentation?"

"Primarily the existence of an irresponsible censorship. The fact that my *Salome* cannot be performed is sufficient to show the folly of such an institution. If painters were obliged to show their pictures to clerks at Somerset House, those who think in form and colour would adopt some other mode of expression. If every novel had to be submitted to a police magistrate, those whose passion is fiction would seek some new mode of realization. No art ever survived censorship; no art ever will."

"And secondly?"

"Secondly to the rumour persistently spread abroad by journalists for the last thirty years, that the duty of the dramatist was to please the public. The aim of art is no more to give pleasure than to give pain. The aim of art is to be art. As I said once before, the work of art is to dominate the spectator – the spectator is not to dominate art."

"You admit no exceptions?"

"Yes. Circuses, where it seems the wishes of the public might be reasonably carried out."

"Do you think," I inquired, "that French dramatic criticism is superior to our own?"

"It would be unfair to confuse French dramatic criticism with English theatrical criticism. The French dramatic critic is always a man of culture and generally a man of letters. In France poets like Gautier[1] have been dramatic critics. In England they are drawn from a less distinguished class. They have neither the same capacities nor the same opportunities. They have all the moral qualities, but none of the artistic qualifications. For the criticism of such a complex mode of art as the drama the highest culture is necessary. No one can criticise drama who is not capable of receiving impressions from the other arts also."

"You admit they are sincere?"

"Yes; but their sincerity is little more than stereotyped stupidity. The critic of the drama should be as versatile as the actor. He should be able to change his mood at will and should catch the colour of the moment."

"At least they are honest?"

"Absolutely. I don't believe there is a single dramatic critic in London who would deliberately set himself to misrepresent the work of any dramatist — unless, of course, he personally disliked the dramatist, or had some play of his own he wished to produce at the same theatre, or had an old friend among the actors, or some natural reasons of that kind. I am speaking, however, of London dramatic critics. In the provinces both audience and critics are cultured. In London it is only the audience who are cultured."

"I fear you do not rate our dramatic critics very highly, Mr Wilde; but, at all events, they are incorruptible?"

"In a market where there are no bidders."

[1] Théophile Gautier, poet and novelist (1811–1872).

191

"Still their memories stand them in good stead," I pleaded.

"The old talk of having seen Macready:[1] that must be a very painful memory. The middle-aged boast that they can recall *Diplomacy*:[2] hardly a pleasant reminiscence."

"You deny them, then, even a creditable past?"

"They have no past and no future, and are incapable of realizing the colour of the moment that finds them at the play."

"What do you propose should be done?"

"They should be pensioned off, and only allowed to write on politics or theology or bimetallism, or some subject easier than art."

"In fact," I said, carried away by Mr Wilde's aphorisms, "they should be seen and not heard."

"The old should neither be seen nor heard," said Mr Wilde, with some emphasis.

"You said the other day there were only two dramatic critics in London.[3] May I ask — "

"They must have been greatly gratified by such an admission from me; but I am bound to say that since last week I have struck one of them from the list."

"Whom have you left in?"

"I think I had better not mention his name. It might

---

[1] William Charles Macready, actor-manager (1793–1873). Friend of Dickens.

[2] A version of Sardou's *Dora* by B.C. Stephenson and Clement Scott, first produced in 1878 and revived in 1884 and 1893. In an interview with Gilbert Burgess, published in the *Sketch* on 9 January 1895, Wilde said "Sardou is not understood in England because he is only known through a rather ordinary travesty of his play *Dora*."

[3] "Are there absolutely no real critics in London?"

"There are just two."

"Who are they?" I asked eagerly.

Mr Wilde, with the elaborate courtesy for which he has always been famous, replied: "I think I had better not mention their names; it might make the others so jealous." (Gilbert Burgess in the *Sketch*.)

make him too conceited. Conceit is the privilege of the creative."

"How would you define ideal dramatic criticism?"

"As far as my work is concerned, unqualified appreciation."

"And whom have you omitted?"

"Mr William Archer, of the *World*."

"What do you chiefly object to in his article?"

"I object to nothing in the article, but I grieve at everything in it. It is bad taste in him to write of me by my Christian name, and he need not have stolen his vulgarisms from the *National Observer* in its most impudent and impotent days."[1]

"Mr Archer asked whether it was agreeable to you to be hailed by your Christian name when the enthusiastic spectators called you before the curtain."

"To be so addressed by enthusiastic spectators is as great a compliment as to be written of by one's Christian name is in a journalist bad manners. Bad manners make a journalist."

"Do you think French actors, like French criticism, superior to our own?"

"The English actors act quite as well; but they act best

[1] In his review of *An Ideal Husband* in the *World*, 9 January 1895, William Archer, the Scottish dramatic critic, playwright, and translator of Ibsen (1856–1924), had said that it could not be agreeable to Wilde "to be familiarly hailed by the gallery as 'Oscar', like a favourite music-hall artist . . . who has just done a screaming 'turn'. My sympathies, however, are entirely with the gallery. They have a perfect right to take him at his own valuation. There are two men behind that enigmatic mask: Oscar and Wilde, the — I had almost said the mountebank — and the artist; and when the worser is predominant, we naturally accord him the treatment he invites." Archer went on to refer to his "esteem and relish" for the artist in Wilde but his distaste for "Oscarism" — the cheap and facile elements in his work. "In this play we drink deeper than ever of Oscarism; we reach its very dregs." Archer soon redeemed himself by a highly favourable review of *The Importance of Being Earnest* in the *World* of 20 February.

between the lines. They lack the superb elocution of the French — so clear, so cadenced, and so musical. A long sustained speech seems to exhaust them. At the Théâtre Français we go to listen, to an English theatre we go to look. There are, of course, exceptions. Mr George Alexander, Mr Lewis Waller, Mr Forbes-Robertson, and others I might mention, have superb voices and know how to use them. I wish I could say the same of the critics; but in the case of the literary drama in England there is too much of what is technically known as 'business'. Yet there is more than one of our English actors who is capable of producing a wonderful dramatic effect by aid of a monosyllable and two cigarettes."

For a moment Mr Wilde was silent, and then added, "Perhaps, after all, that is acting."

"But are you satisfied with the interpreters of *An Ideal Husband*?"

"I am charmed with all of them. Perhaps they are a little too fascinating. The stage is the refuge of the too fascinating."

"Have you heard it said that all the characters in your play talk as you do?"

"Rumours of that kind have reached me from time to time," said Mr Wilde, lighting a cigarette, "and I should fancy that some such criticism has been made. The fact is that it is only in the last few years that the dramatic critic has had the opportunity of seeing plays written by anyone who has a mastery of style. In the case of a dramatist also an artist it is impossible not to feel that the work of art, to be a work of art, must be dominated by the artist. Every play of Shakespeare is dominated by Shakespeare. Ibsen and Dumas dominate their works. My works are dominated by myself."

"Have you ever been influenced by any of your predecessors?"

"It is enough for me to state definitely, and I hope once for all, that not a single dramatist in this century has ever in

194

the smallest degree influenced me. Only two have interested me."

"And they are?"

"Victor Hugo and Maeterlinck."

"Other writers surely have influenced your other works?"

"Setting aside the prose and poetry of Greek and Latin
authors, the only writers who have influenced me are Keats,
Flaubert, and Walter Pater; and before I came across them
I had already gone more than half-way to meet them. Style
must be in one's soul before one can recognize it in others."

"And do you consider *An Ideal Husband* the best of your
plays?"

A charming smile crossed Mr Wilde's face.

"Have you forgotten my classical expression — that only
mediocrities improve?[1] My three plays are to each other, as a
wonderful young poet has beautifully said,

> — as one white rose
> On one green stalk, to another one.[2]

They form a perfect cycle, and in their delicate sphere complete both life and art."

"Do you think that the critics will understand your new
play, which Mr George Alexander has secured?"

"I hope not."

"I dare not ask, I suppose, if it will please the public?"

"When a play that is a work of art is produced on the
stage, what is being tested is not the play, but the stage;
when a play that is *not* a work of art is produced on the stage
what is being tested is not the play, but the public."

"What sort of play are we to expect?"

---

[1] "Only mediocrities progress. An artist revolves in a cycle of masterpieces" (Wilde to the Editor of the *Pall Mall Gazette*, 22 September
1894, see *Letters*, p. 372).
[2] Lord Alfred Douglas, "Jonquil and Fleur de Lys", published in his
*Poems* (1896).

"It is exquisitely trivial, a delicate bubble of fancy, and it has its philosophy."

"Its philosophy?"

"That we should treat all the trivial things of life very seriously, and all the serious things of life with sincere and studied triviality."

"You have no leanings towards realism?"

"None whatever. Realism is only a background; it cannot form an artistic motive for a play that is to be a work of art."

"Still I have heard you congratulated on your pictures of London society."

"If Robert Chiltern, the Ideal Husband, were a common clerk, the humanity of his tragedy would be none the less poignant. I have placed him in the higher ranks of life merely because that is the side of social life with which I am best acquainted. In a play dealing with actualities to write with ease one must write with knowledge."

"Then you see nothing suggestive of treatment in the tragedies of every-day existence?"

"If a journalist is run over by a four-wheeler in the Strand, an incident I regret to say I have never witnessed, it suggests nothing to me from a dramatic point of view. Perhaps I am wrong; but the artist must have his limitations."

"Well," I said, rising to go, "I have enjoyed myself immensely."

"I was sure you would," said Mr Wilde. "But tell me how you manage your interviews."

"Oh, Pitman," I said carelessly.

"Is that your name? It's not a very *nice* name."

Then I left.

# APPENDIX B

## A REMINISCENCE OF 1898[1]

### by Wilfred Hugh Chesson[2]

After 16 Tite Street, Chelsea, had been ransacked and despoiled to pay his creditors, a resident of 5 Tite Street, Chelsea, entered a bookshop in the adjacent Queen's Road. That resident was I. There I bought Wilde's beribboned Bible, some leaves of his manuscripts, the copy of Shakespeare's Sonnets which he had studied before writing *Mr W.H.*, a private copy of *The Duchess of Padua*, and a corrected copy of *Vera; or, The Nihilists*, a tragedy which he wrote when he was eighteen. The find was a happy one, enabling me to penetrate into his workshop.

In 1898 I wrote to Wilde, offering him the plays as a gift. His reply reached me in Paris. It told me that his name was henceforth Sebastian Melmoth, and I saw that he had borrowed from a horrible romance which half Europe once admired, but which he was too modern to care much about.

---

[1] Published in the December 1911 issue of the New York *Bookman*. I have omitted the first three paragraphs, which do not refer to the visit.
[2] Novelist and critic (1870–1952). In 1894 he and Edward Garnett were the principal readers of the publisher T. Fisher Unwin, and when in 1894 a manuscript was submitted for Unwin's Pseudonym Library under the name Kamudi, Chesson was the first person to read *Almayer's Folly*. With Garnett's enthusiastic approval, he recommended it for publication. Conrad said that if *Almayer's Folly* had been rejected he would never have written another book, so lovers of Conrad owe a great deal to Chesson (see an explanatory article by Ugo Mursia in *Conradiana*, Vol IV, No 2, 1972, published at the Texas Tech University at Lubbock, Texas).

In 1897 Chesson was the original reader and recommender of Somerset Maugham's first novel *Liza of Lambeth*.

I mean *Melmoth the Wanderer*, by Charles Maturin, a connection of Wilde's family.

Wilde's Paris address was Hôtel d'Alsace, Rue des Beaux-Arts, and there I delivered *The Duchess of Padua* and some leaves of his manuscripts. He was staying, however, at L'Idée, Perreux, Nogent-sur-Marne, and thence he sent me an invitation to breakfast.

On 5 July 1898 — a perfect summer day — I saw for the first time, except in *Punch*, the tall and debonair poet and wit, who, in adversity, had entered my Pantheon. He awaited me at the gate of the courtyard of L'Idée — an unaffected Englishman, stalwart in homespun.

"I am correcting the proofs of a play," he said. "*The Importance of Being Earnest.*" He gave good Irish weight, without roll, to the syllable "port", and I was amused, for I knew that he was throwing the play into the title.

We sat *vis-à-vis* at a round table in the courtyard, and I noticed the massiveness of his hair, and thought how different was its thick but not wavy abundance from the operatic idea of flowing locks. I hoped, as my eyes fell on his proofs, on a table near us, that he felt creative and eager for art. I named a man who borrowed his style in affecting to satirise it, and asked if such a person were not enough to irritate him into the mood for writing more novels and plays.

"It is dreadful, is it not?" he said, *apropos* the imitations of him thrown upon the market. "Of course I can write, but I have lost the joy of writing."

I praised the future, and he said piously, "I do not doubt that there are as wonderful things in my future as there are in my past."

I told him my impression of *The Ballad of Reading Gaol*. "Ah! I had to write that," he said, as if it came as naturally as the eloquent letters upon children in Reading Gaol which appeared in the *Daily Chronicle* after his release. "I am glad," I said, "that you allowed yourself a bad rhyme.

198

'We banged the tins and bawled the hymns' is so perfectly out of tune." He said he had thought of revising the line, but a friend had persuaded him to retain it. He thought the press had noticed the poem "very sweetly," and quoted a phrase by Mr Arthur Symons — "the unseen violence upon souls." "I should love to have written it," he said. This unseen violence was the only personal suffering in prison which he spoke about.

"Once," he said, "while we were exercising, a man behind me said, 'This is a strange place to meet Dorian Gray in!' 'Not Dorian Gray,' I said, 'but Lord Henry Wotton.' " Lord Henry, in *The Picture of Dorian Gray*, is Dorian's instructor in pleasure. "This man," added Wilde, "had mastered, as we all had to, the art of talking without moving the lips. He said, 'I was at all your first nights, and I was at your trials.' "

Wilde spoke with kindness of the associates of C. 3. 3.,[1] and here and there admired. "Have you ever noticed a thief's hands?" he asked, "how beautiful they are? How fine and delicate at the tips? They must be fine and delicate to take the watch from your pocket without your knowing." His own hands were large and thick, and one of them was adorned by a scarab as big as a sixpence. "They say it is unlucky to wear it," he said: "but it is thousands of years old. I kept it when the rest went."

He told me that, after his release, he went to a palmist in Paris. She looked at his hands and said, "I am puzzled. By your line of life you died two years ago. I cannot explain the fact except by supposing that since then you have been living on your line of imagination."

Having some knowledge of the cheiromantic art, I looked at his left hand. "Here," I said, indicating a horizontal

---

[1] Wilde's number in Reading Gaol. It appeared as the author's name in the first six editions of *The Ballad*. After that Wilde's name was added in brackets.

under the little finger, "is the line of your marriage."

"That, too, was a fatality," he murmured.

Of two prison governors with whom he had to do, he said that the former was not able to enjoy his breakfast unless someone was punished before he ate it: of the other he said, "He was the most Christ-like man I ever met."

Snatcher, a lively dog lent to him by Mr Rowland Strong, was present and eagerly snapped up a morsel which Wilde rendered more appetising by christening it Dreyfus.[1] He told me that he knew Esterhazy,[2] and said that that remarkable man had said that at the age of thirteen he had a profound conviction that he would never be happy again as long as he lived. "And it was quite true; he never was," Wilde added.

We went for a long walk by the pleasant river Marne: and I was touched when the exile said, "Might not this be a bit of the Thames?" Delightful residences rose on our right, and at a tall gate, which suggested rather than disclosed one of them, Wilde paused and said, "That is what I like, just to stand and peep through the bars. It would be better than being in Paradise to stand like this, catch a glimpse as now, and want to go in. The reality would be sure to be disappointing."

We talked literature, and he told me stories from Guy de Maupassant with enchanting energy. Thus it was that I heard of the two malcontents who, after all their grumbling,

[1] Strong had been violently anti-Dreyfus when he was training the dog, but then discovered Esterhazy's guilt and changed his mind. The dog had clearly not followed suit.

[2] Commandant Marie-Charles Walsin-Esterhazy (1847–1923) was the man who forged the famous document, known as the *bordereau*, for which Dreyfus was sentenced to exile on Devil's Island. Wilde's friend and translator Henry D. Davray reported Wilde as saying of Esterhazy: *"C'est lui qui est l'auteur du bordereau, il me l'a avoué . . . Esterhazy est bien plus intéressant que Dreyfus qui est innocent. On a toujours tort d'être innocent. Pour être criminel, il faut de l'imagination et du courage. . . . Mais c'est fâcheux qu'Esterhazy ne soit jamais allé en prison."*

preferred to be shot rather than divulge the password to the besiegers of Paris.[1] He said that he had been struck by the power of a drama he had seen acted in a French theatre patronised both by criminals who wished to see an actor in a criminal role and men of letters interested in an artistic production. The point of the drama was the betrayal of a ferocious murderer by a timid light-of-love with whom he spent his last hours of freedom. There is a reward for his capture, and the girl is pressed by a hag to earn it. The murderer is taken in his sleep, and as, hopelessly over-powered, he is borne away, his hatred of his betrayer goes out in one venomous look. She sees it, and his impotence, the absolute certainty of his doom, are nothing to her. *"J'ai peur, j'ai peur!"* she shrieks, and the curtain falls. Wilde delivered these words with a force that went into the marrow of my bones.

The subject of fear made him talk of the guillotine, which he had seen operate in the early morning. "I have seen the victim look green with fright," he said. "They are kind to him up to the last minute. He may smoke a cigarette as he goes to the Place de la Roquette, but once there, what a change! They are on him like tigers, and his head is thrust into the groove under the knife as if he were not a man at all."

He spoke of the Morgue. "It is a dignified place. I cannot understand why people should object to go to it. There is nothing horrible in death. Death is solemn. Now waxworks are horrible, if you like. I remember," he proceeded, "going to the Morgue after seeing a brilliant function — all colour and music — at Notre Dame. A woman of the lowest class was on one of the slabs. She was having her day. All Paris might look at her gravely. She was no longer despised."

He grew gay when, in addition to finding a franc for a *cannette* of beer, I found matches for our cigarettes. "You

---

[1] *"Deux Amis"* from Maupassant's volume *Mademoiselle Fifi*. It is not clear whether the grumblers knew the password or not.

are perfect," he said. "It was good when you produced money, and now you produce matches. What more can you ask of life?"

More, of course, could be asked, but my requisition waited while he told me of a silver matchbox he once had. It was stolen by a Neapolitan boy. Taxed with the theft, the culprit confessed. "You must give it up," said Wilde. "I cannot," was the reply. "It is too beautiful." "Come, come, where is it?" insisted the owner of the matchbox. "I have hidden it," said the boy. "Every night I look at it before I sleep. I have never been so happy." At last Wilde pleaded that the matchbox was a souvenir from a dear friend. The boy was sceptical. There must be no fibbing. "Are you sure?" Wilde was sure, upon his honour, and the boy's heart was moved.

We dined in the courtyard of L'Idée, and talked more literature. "Do you know," asked Wilde, "who destroyed the manuscript of Carlyle's *French Revolution*?" "The servant of John Stuart Mill," I replied, as informed by biographies. "It was finer than that," said he. "It was Mrs Mill. She read it and saw at once that, if it was published, the first name in nineteenth-century English literature could not be John Stuart Mill. It would be Carlyle. Think of it. What servant could destroy the manuscript of a whole volume in lighting a kitchen fire? She could only burn a few pages at a time, and be found out long before the end. No, it was Mrs Mill. But her heroism was wasted. She had not reckoned on Carlyle's marvellous memory. How great he was! He made history a song for the first time in our language. He was our English Tacitus."

He spoke with enthusiasm of Dickens. Micawber, Pecksniff, Mrs Gamp, flitted before us. "There have been no such grotesques since the Gothic gargoyles," he said, and he quoted the passage in *Martin Chuzzlewit* which compares the rusty gowns and other garments hanging from Sarah

Gamp's bed to "guardian angels" watching her in her sleep.

He spoke with affectionate amusement of Mr J.B. Yeats, Senior.[1] "Do you know how he became a painter? It was so simple and natural. He was a thriving barrister, when one day he came down to breakfast and said, 'Children, I am tired of the law, and shall become a painter.' They said, 'Papa is going to be a painter,' and were quite happy."

"Could he paint?" I asked.

"Not in the least; that was the beauty of it," said Wilde.

He could, however, as I discovered when I was in the dining-room of Mr and Mrs Hinkson and saw his portrait of Katharine Tynan's[2] father.

Wilde expressed much amusement at Mr W.M. Rossetti's family publications. He understood, I know not with what authority, that Christina Rossetti's washing-book had been given to the public, and supposed that historical piety could go no further. He diverted me by a parody of Mr Rossetti's account of his brother's misunderstanding with a bird. The poet, it appears, was much annoyed, and explained that a thrush was saying ill-natured things about him in the garden. "But as far as I could gather," Wilde represented Mr Rossetti as remarking, "the bird's observations had nothing to do with my brother."[3]

"Tell me about 'Jameson's Raid', " he said. "I am told it was very funny," and I quoted a line here and there from Mr Austin's refreshing song.[4] He begged for a copy of it, and it is on my conscience that I never sent him one. By way of

[1] John Butler Yeats (1839–1922), father of the poet.
[2] Irish poet and novelist (1861–1931), married M.A. Hinkson in 1883.
[3] See *Letters*, p. 520.
[4] Alfred Austin (1835–1913), recently appointed Poet Laureate, published his poem "Jameson's Raid" in *The Times* on 11 January 1896. It commemorated the defeat by the Boers of Dr Leander Starr Jameson's disastrous raid on 2 January 1896. The poem begins:
> Wrong! Is it wrong? Well, may be:
> But I'm going, boys, all the same.

conversation I wondered how the laureateship was support-able in a sleet of ridicule. "Vanity, my dear sir," he replied. "Vanity, the invulnerable breastplate of man."

"Why didn't they make Kipling the laureate?" he asked. "It would have been such a change, so artistic. There was Tennyson, with his idylls, his well-bred and dainty muse, and here is Kipling, who makes his muse say 'Go to hell.' " He commented sarcastically on Mr Kipling's encyclopaedic method. "I object to know all about cod-fishing," he re-marked.[1] He spoke with enthusiasm of some of Mr Kipling's poetry, and quoted two well-known passages for the sake of their metaphor. "An' the dawn comes up like thunder" was one of them. The other he gave as one who rejoices. "He trod the ling like a buck in spring, and he looked like a lance in rest."[2]

Swinburne he termed "mere froth of the sea", meaning high praise, perhaps. He said he was the first English poet to sing divinely the song of the flesh. We did not speak of Donne, Carew, Herrick, who were so much more minute in their praise of women. He spoke with aversion of Matthew Arnold's snippety sonnets: the adjective is mine. He said that he read through the whole of Dante's *Divina Com-media* in prison. "You can imagine," he said, "how I tasted every word." He recommended me to read it in Long-fellow's rhymed translation, preferring it to Cary's dull blank verse. I mentioned Verhaeren, and he immediately said, "Oh! now you mention the greatest living poet."[3]

He spoke of old friends — of Mr Frank Harris, a man who does not think that a murmur of "poor fellow" suffices to attest his sympathy for a friend in trouble; of "dear Max",[4] whose caricature of him I cannot imagine. Of Sir Charles

[1] Kipling's *Captains Courageous* was published in 1897.
[2] From "Mandalay" and "The Ballad of East and West".
[3] Emile Verhaeren, Belgian poet (1855–1916).
[4] Max Beerbohm, writer and caricaturist (1872–1956).

Dilke[1] he said: "I've only one fault to find with Dilke; he knows too much about everything. It is hard to have a good story interrupted by a fact. I admit accuracy up to a certain point, but Dilke's accuracy is almost a vice."

Of Henley, whom I found a sympathetic critic, he spoke more harshly than of any one except a prison governor. "Have you noticed," he observed, "that if a man has once been an editor he can always be an editor? The fact that a paper has a way of dying when he is on it is of the smallest importance. He is in demand before the corpse is buried. There is Henley. He kills the *Scots Observer*. Hey presto! he is made editor of the *New Review*. Then the *New Review* dies."

He had not yet done with the author of *London Voluntaries*; his next remark was a voluntary of sensational vigour: "The man," he said, "is simply eaten up with envy of any man whom he has not discovered. Fame exists on this condition: Henley must have made it." For me, of whom Henley had written that he read me "with unwonted interest", this was simple Esperanto, and I was pleased when Wilde descanted upon envy as distinct from henvy. It is very wrong; it is unintellectual, he said.[2]

The night was warm, and we stayed in the darkened courtyard. The eyes of Oscar Wilde grew very bright and he gazed with devotional rapture into his own day.

"My work was a joy to me," he said. "I wrote *Dorian Gray* in three weeks. When my plays were on, I drew a hundred pounds a week! I delighted in every minute of the day."

[1] 1843–1911. Radical M.P. whose political career was ruined by his appearance as co-respondent in a divorce case in 1885.
[2] Henley had grown steadily more antagonistic to Wilde and his work, and had ended by writing an unfavourable review of *The Ballad* in the *Outlook*. For Wilde's amusing paragraph about him in 1897 see *Letters*, p. 631.

He told me to read *Mes Communions*, by Georges Eek-houd,[1] a story of friendship ending in disaster worse than his, and he spoke that story to me in thrilling English, which returned to me when I read it in French, and is in me yet.

The implacable Old Bailey rose before me as I looked at him, and again I waited for a verdict which would be upon Art as well as a man. I remembered a verdict which set Wilde free in an atmosphere of dread, and I remembered Lockwood's stentorian oration on a Saturday when I waited alone in a house of the street where he had lived.[2] I remembered the brute force of judgment which banged the books of Scott and Dickens upon this man's writing. I remembered his infernal Sabbath after the second jury had spoken. I remembered a thriving comedy which Mr Alexander had put on without its author's name, and I remembered, as one remembers rhetoric, that Lockwood was dead and that Mr Alexander had known what it was to be criminally slandered and to encounter the professionally sceptical gaze of a magistrate.[3]

---

[1] Flemish writer (1854–1927). See *Letters*, p. 814.

[2] Sir Frank Lockwood (1847–97), the Solicitor General, led for the prosecution in Wilde's second trial. In his long *De Profundis* letter of 1897 (*Letters*, p. 502) Wilde wrote: "I remember as I was sitting in the dock . . . listening to Lockwood's appalling denunciation of me — like a thing out of Tacitus, like a passage in Dante, like one of Savonarola's indictments of the Popes at Rome — and being sickened with horror at what I heard."

[3] Early in the morning of 4 November 1895 George Alexander was arrested with a female prostitute in a Chelsea street. Later in the morning he was brought before a magistrate, who, despite incriminating evidence from the police and admissions from the lady (Alexander claimed that on being accosted he had given her half-a-crown out of charity), gave him the benefit of the doubt and he was discharged. On 7 November the *Daily Chronicle* published a letter from Bernard Shaw, in which he claimed that "the circumstance, described by Mr Alexander up to the point of the intervention of the policeman have occurred to me more than once".

I gave Wilde the gleams of my thought; he was indifferent. "When I came out," he said, "my friends presented me with a box full of beautiful books — Keats, and so on. They are at Naples. There they lie." He looked at me. "You worry too much: never worry"; and he talked again like an habitué of Hatchard's. "I do not approve of the shape of the Pseudonym Library," he said. "It is too narrow.[1] It is unjust to a good style to print it on a tiny page. Imagine turning Pater over rapidly. It is violence."

I reminded him of his relative, the Rev. E.J. Hardy,[2] one of the Pseudonym publisher's great successes. "Ah, yes, he has got on. I reviewed *How to be Happy though Married* for the *Pall Mall*, and I called it 'The Murray of Matrimony and the Baedeker of Bliss'. I used to say that I should have received a royalty for that phrase."

I could not refrain from returning to his own work. While we were out I saw him as the big friend of a pretty French child, whom he had bought a toy for at a fair. I knew he was cut off from his own children. I knew that bright work could be a populous world for him in his lonely histrionic life. He told me in response that his work was in his head; he did not write it down. Then he related to me this parable:

"A man saw a being, which hid its face from him, and he said, 'I will compel it to show its face.' It fled as he pursued, and he lost it, and his life went on. At last his pleasure drew him into a long room, where tables were spread for many, and in a mirror he saw the being whom he had pursued in youth. 'This time you shall not escape me!' he cried, but the being did not try to escape, and hid its face no more. 'Look!' it cried, 'and now you will know that we cannot see each

---

[1] Its pages measured $6\frac{3}{4}$ inches down and $3\frac{1}{2}$ inches across.
[2] The Rev. Edward John Hardy (1849–1920) was an assistant master at Portora Royal School when Wilde was a pupil there. He married a niece of Sir William Wilde. Wilde reviewed his book in the *Pall Mall Gazette* on 18 November 1885.

other again, for this is the face of your own soul, and it is horrible.' "

The flash of rhetoric over, he grew sympathetic and looked at my fingers persuasively. "You worry too much," he said. "Never worry." I touched on religion, which I considered a killjoy and painmaker, as I do now. I recalled to him his remark to Wilberforce[1] that the chief argument against Christianity is the style of St Paul. "I fear he tempted me," he said. "There is really something very artistic about Christianity," he said. "You go into Hyde Park, and a wonderful sentence comes to you on the wind. 'What shall it profit a man if he gain the whole world and lose his own soul?' "

I spoke of life in spirit. He became indignant. "There is no hell but this," he said; "a body without a soul, or a soul without a body."

It was about ten of the night when he went with me to the railway station. I said that his life was a harmony of two extremes, very rare and I thought very valuable. With a level suavity that, like the lawns of Oxford, had centuries of culture behind it, he replied, "Yes, artistically it is perfect; socially most inconvenient." We parted on a gay note, "It does not matter what class you go in up to Paris."

---

[1] Possibly Canon Basil Wilberforce (1841–1916), who was a friend and protégé of Lady Mount-Temple.

# INDEX OF RECIPIENTS

Le Gallienne, Richard, 97, 120
Lewis, Mrs George, 41
Lucy, Henry, 80, 84

Macmillan, George, 31, 70, 80
Marbury, Elisabeth, 119, 122
Marillier, H.C., 58, 59, 60, 63
Mathews, Elkin, 116, 117, 126
Maxse, Leo, 123
McCarthy, Justin Huntly, 82
Medhurst, Blanche, 73
Merivale, Mrs H.C., 57
Merrill, Stuart, 102
Millais, Mrs, 54
Monaco, Princess Alice of, 95
Morris, May, 82
Morse, Col. W.F., 42, 46

Nash, Harry, 55
Norton, Charles Eliot, 41
Nutt, Alfred, 102

O'Reilly, John Boyle, 47
Oxford Union, Librarian of, 36

*Pall Mall Gazette*, editor of, 56
Pickering, Arthur Howard, 89
Pigott, E.F.S., 32

Raynaud, Ernest, 101
Rehan, Ada, 182
Reid, Wemyss, 67, 72, 86
Richards, Mrs, 73
Richards, S. Wall, 65
Ricketts, Charles, 123
Robins, Elizabeth, 79
Rodd, Rennell, 33
Rose, Edward, 147

Ross, Robert, 128, 153, 171, 183, 184
Royal Academy Students, 53

Salisbury, Marchioness of, 71
Sarrazin, Gabriel, 60
*Scots Observer*, editor of, 88
Scott, Clement, 34
Sherard, Robert, 103, 107
Sladen, Douglas, 77
Smithers, Leonard, 157, 159, 160, 167, 168, 169, 170, 171, 173, 175, 177, 178, 179, 180, 181
Stead, W.T., 78
Sterner, Albert, 101
Stoddart, J.M., 45, 87
Stoker, Florence,. 73
Stoker & Hansell, Messrs, 133
Strangman, Edward, 149, 150, 172, 174
Strong, Rowland, 166

Terry, Ellen, 68
Terry, Fred, 127
Tree, Herbert Beerbohm, 118
Turner, Reginald, 151

Unidentified Correspondents, 23, 31, 87, 115, 129, 133, 174

Vian, Alsagar, 66, 68
Vice-Chancellor of Oxford University, 26

Ward, Samuel, 48
Watson, Homer, 72
Wilde, Oscar, 35, 117, 124, 125, 129, 143, 185

# GENERAL INDEX

Adey, More, 134, 136, 138, 139, 140, 141, 142, 161, 165
Aeschylus, 34
Alexander, George, 109, 112, 130, 136, 148, 173, 175, 179, 194, 195, 206
Anderson, Joseph, 99, 104
Anderson, Mary, 85
Appleton, G.W., 56
Archer, William, 193
Aristides, 38
Arnold, Matthew, 204
Austin, Alfred, 203
Aveling, Eleanor Marx, 83

Bale, Edwin, 86
Balfour, Arthur, 96
Balfour, Lady Betty, 99
*Ballad of Reading Gaol, The*, 150, 157, 158, 159, 165, 166, 167, 168, 169, 170, 171, 198
Balzac, 148
Barlas, John, 108, 109
Barrett, Lawrence, 85, 91, 104
Barrymore, Maurice, 119
Beardsley, Aubrey, 151, 170, 175, 177
Beaumont Trust, 61–62
Beerbohm, Max, 204
Beere, Mrs Bernard, 32, 133
Bellew, Kyrle, 182, 186
Benson, F.R., 34

Bigelow, Mrs John, 49
Blakeney, Mrs, 45
Bobbie, *see* Ross
Booth, Agnes, 120
Bosie, *see* Douglas
Boucicault, Mr & Mrs Dion, 50
Brown Potter, Cora, 182, 185
Browning, Oscar, 74
Buchanan, Robert, 68
Burgess, Gilbert, 192
Burnand, F.C., 35
Burne-Jones, Edward, 41

Calhoun, Eleanor, 85–86
Callan (unidentified), 170
Campbell, Lady Archie, 70
Carlyle, Thomas, 160, 202
Carr, Joseph Comyns, 80, 81
Catullus, 158
Champion, H.H., 108
Chesson, W.H., 197–208
Clifton, Arthur, 76, 114, 162, 179
Coghlan, Rose, 122
Conder, Charles, 151
Conrad, Joseph, 197
Cook, E.T., 64
Cook, Keningale, 25
Corkran, Alice, 78
Courtney, W.L., 96, 34
Cowper, Lady, 98, 99
Craik, Mrs, 71
Crane, Walter, 73

211

215